# HOW
# TO
# DESIGN
# A
# GARDEN

# HOW TO

Create and maintain
your dream garden

# DESIGN

Pollyanna
Wilkinson

# A

# GARDEN

# CONTENTS

# WELCOME TO GARDEN DESIGN

Hello, dear reader. Do you have a garden? Do you want to design it? Then this is the garden design book for you. Now, let's get one thing straight right away – this book isn't a textbook. It's the book equivalent of sitting down with your friend (not just any friend – your well-qualified friend) over a glass of wine or a cup of tea to talk about your garden, figure out what you want it to look like and how you want to use it, and then plan it together.

I am going to give you all the information you need and, hopefully, not send you either to sleep or into a state of terror. I want you to be excited about the prospect of a beautiful garden that is completely tailored to your needs, and I promise to be brutally honest about design features I love and hate – some of which may be controversial. And hey, we're going to keep things practical too, because your garden needs to be beautiful *and* useful. So what are we waiting for – shall we design your garden?

Generous borders flank this casual seating space and provide a wow-factor view from the house.

1

# WHAT DO YOU WANT FROM YOUR GARDEN?

YOUR NEEDS AND WANTS, WISHLIST, THE LOOK AND FEEL, MOODBOARD, AND PRACTICALITIES

In this chapter, we're going to start by establishing your brief. Your brief is essentially a summary of how you want to use your garden and what features you'd like to include, as well as how you might want it to look and feel. We're going to consider practical elements such as budget and maintenance, as well as timeframes and aesthetics. By the end of this chapter, you should have a clear idea of what you want and be one step closer to designing your dream garden.

# UNDERSTANDING WHAT YOU WANT AND NEED

So where do we start? Whenever I meet a new client for the first time, the very first question I ask is *how* do you want to use your garden? And you should now ask yourself this very same thing. It can be a daunting question to answer, but the priority here is to create a list of uses that are realistic and in line with your lifestyle, budget, and, importantly, appetite for maintenance.

## How do you want to use your garden?

From my perspective, I like to think I will waft about my garden brimming with plants, in a kaftan and sipping champagne, hosting sumptuous feasts cooked outdoors each weekend, while also tending an extensive cutting garden and borders deeper than those at Sissinghurst. But the cold, hard reality is infinitely more ordinary. At this stage in my life, I have two children who like to play football, so a lawn is essential. I also run a business full time, and so my leisure time to tend said borders and cutting garden is limited. To that end, my garden needs to be a careful balance of plant filled and beautiful (for me), while also being family friendly (for my kids). What about you? Have a think about your lifestyle and what you need your garden to be for you and how you will realistically use it.

I say this not to sound like an enormous killjoy, but to encourage a healthy dose of realism alongside aspiration when considering your uses, to ensure a garden that works for you. This doesn't mean it will not be beautiful – far from it – but to paraphrase William Morris, everything in your garden needs to be either beautiful or useful (or ideally both). So, let's dive deeper into the *uses* of your garden. Resist the urge to think about aesthetics – that comes later. All we want to focus on now is *how* you will use it. So, let's look at some questions to ponder to get started.

Seating areas are a vital component of a garden, and I try to include several throughout a garden to maximize the use of space.

## STARTER QUESTIONS

- Do you want to dine in the garden?

- Do you want to cook in it?

- Do you want somewhere to relax that isn't a dining space?

- Will children and/or pets need space to play?

- Do you want to escape off into a quiet corner to read, meditate, or hide from the family (I'm half joking)?

- Do you want to sunbathe in complete privacy?

- Do you want to exercise in it? If so, how?

- Would you like a work space in the garden?

- Do you plan to entertain in the garden or is it your private sanctuary?

- Would you like to use it year-round or just in the summer months?

- Do you want to actually garden in your garden?

- Do you want to grow fruit and vegetables?

- Are you keen to support wildlife?

There are probably many other questions to ask, but this should get you thinking about how you use your space. How you use your garden is entirely based on your lifestyle and those you live with, so tailor this list specifically to your needs and uses. Also, if you live with a partner, then I suggest you both make your own list and compare notes. You wouldn't believe how often the priorities of a couple differ, so it's best to be in agreement about what are the most important uses before moving on.

So now you have your list of uses. Perhaps you plan to spend much of your time sunbathing in the nude (no judgment or tan lines here), so from this we can deduce privacy is going to be key. Or perhaps you love to host big groups of people at the weekend, in which case, plenty of space to entertain is essential. Or maybe your garden is your sanctuary and you love to potter in it, in which case, let's get you some cut flowerbeds and some generous borders to tend (yum). We will keep coming back to your wishlist, so keep it handy.

## Who will use your garden?

This feeds into your how, but you also want to consider *who* is using your garden when you're working on your wishlist. If it's just you, then you have the delightful luxury of only having your own needs to consider, but invariably others may also use your garden, from partners and children to extended family, pets, and maintenance services. It's worth just making a note if there are specific factors that are going to inform decisions. This can range from ensuring the garden is accessible for all those with disabilities to making sure there is space for kids and pets to play. And don't forget to think about services that need access, say, to septic or gas tanks, or tree surgeons with large machinery and gardeners with ride-on mowers.

# How long will you have this garden?

The next question to ask yourself is how long will this garden be yours? What you do with your garden is going to be quite different if you are renting (in which case, I'd recommend more moveable solutions such as planting in containers, rather than anything permanent that you can't take with you), versus owning and planning to stay for a handful of years, or spending a lifetime there. This question often freaks people out because it forces them to think about the future, but again, being realistic is always useful. If you are in what you hope will be your "forever home", then your designs should focus on long-term rather than short-term use. It also means what you spend on your garden is largely irrelevant, so long as you can afford it.

If, however, you have another move or two in you, then there are different factors at play. You will likely want to be more judicious with what you spend to ensure you get value for money, and your design can focus more on how you will use the garden in the shorter time you will live there. If a house sale is on the cards, even if it's five to ten years away, it's wise to consider whether the design will appeal to future buyers – and that doesn't mean do nothing! People can be just as put off by a garden that hasn't been "done" if they don't have the appetite for build work as they can by a garden that is totally opposed to their tastes, so it's worth keeping an eye on the style of design. If the garden is more short term, it may be wise to avoid any features that might scare some people away, such as a massive open water feature, which will put off the parents of young children with safety concerns.

# What do you need in your garden?

So, we have dealt with the how and who. Now we need to figure out what you need in the garden, from the uber-practical to the gorgeously aspirational. Ask yourself what you need in your garden for it to be not only useful but also, just as importantly, enjoyable for you.

When compiling your wishlist (see overleaf for some ideas to get you started), it's really important you are realistic with what you can feasibly fit into your garden as well as what you are willing and able to pay for. If you have a small space, you need to be very restrained – and *I promise you*, your garden will look so much better for it. Even if you have a large space and an unlimited budget, don't go crazy ticking everything. I find the very best gardens aren't those that have everything in the list (this can feel very busy indeed), but those that are restrained, considered, and do fewer things really, really well.

## GARDEN WISHLIST

When compiling your wishlist, it's important you are realistic
with what you can feasibly fit into your garden. If your space
is limited, then work with the "less is more" rule.

### WATER

Hot tub
Ice bath
Outdoor shower
Pond or lake
Swimming pool or pond
Water feature

### SPORTS

Basketball hoop
Cricket nets
Croquet lawn
Outdoor gym
    equipment
Petanque/boules pitch
Putting green
Sports pitch
Tennis court
Weight-training space
Yoga platform

### STRUCTURES

Arbour
Carport
Folly or gazebo
Garden office
Greenhouse
Observatory
Pergola
Pool house
Potting shed
Sauna
Sculpture
Storage sheds

### ENTERTAINING AND LEISURE

Argentinian grill
Dining area
Fire pit or fireplace
Hammock
Outdoor kitchen
Pizza oven
Seating area
Standalone BBQ

### FOR THE KIDS

Bike or running trails
Climbing frame
Dens
Playhouse
Sports pitch
Swings
Teepee
Trampoline
Treehouse
Zip wire

### GARDEN FEATURES

Borders
Cut flowerbeds
Fruit cages
Herb garden
Maze
Meadow
Orchard
Rockery
Stumpery (decorative
    tree stumps)
Vegetable beds
Walled garden
Woodland

### FOR WILDLIFE

Beehives
Birdbaths
Bird feeders
Hedgehog houses
Insect hotels
Log piles
Nest boxes
Wildflowers

### UTILITIES

AC or air source heat
    pump units
Animal enclosure
Bike store
Bin store
Car charger
Car parking spaces
Compost area
Dog washer
Fences or walls
Log store
Oil tanks
Outdoor taps
Speakers
Washing line
Water butt

Think about how you want to use your
garden when compiling your wishlist.

# THE LOOK AND FEEL

We're now going to explore the look, feel, and mood of the garden, and there are various ways to do this. I once heard of a designer who asked their clients to close their eyes and imagine how they would feel in their garden. They asked them to pretend to walk through their new garden, smell the flowers, bask in the sunshine, feel the wind in their hair, and so on. Now with no disrespect at all towards my fellow designer (because it really is a lovely idea if you are into this approach), if I were the client here, I would be squirming.

I would be sniggering my way through this exercise because I am a cynic at heart and it's just not my bag. I want to focus more on the use, the aesthetic, and the practicalities. That said, despite my personal feelings on the exercise, the designer was on to something – establishing the mood of the garden is not to be ignored.

## Creating a mood

Anyway, while I'm not going to walk you through a guided meditation on your garden (come on, we both know I am not your girl for this), how a garden makes you feel is just as important as what it looks like, so let's delve a little deeper into this. If you are not so romantically minded, or the thought of this question makes you cringe, feel free to move right along to the next section.

So – feelings. Much like interiors, garden spaces can impact your mood. They can elicit feelings from calming to energizing, from peaceful and connected to the earth, to spiritual, meditative, playful, and motivated. There are so many positive emotions that can be inspired by your garden, and the design will influence this.

For example, when we look at a planting scheme, a border of hot, bright colours can feel invigorating and energizing, whereas a palette of cool whites and pastels immediately feels more tranquil and calm. Equally, the shapes and materials we use in the garden can make us feel differently: a sinuous, curved path or a beautiful, cobbled courtyard are going to feel romantic and whimsical, while a highly structural garden with crisp lines and bold architectural planting is going to feel more formal and serious.

So have a think and ask yourself (or if you feel so inclined, close your eyes and imagine), when you step out into your garden at various times of the year, how do you want to feel? Jot the answers down and keep them in your list of must-haves.

Abundant planting in shades of purple and dark pink creates a soft, romantic feel in this country garden and a welcoming approach to the back door.

WHAT DO YOU WANT FROM YOUR GARDEN?

WHAT DO YOU WANT FROM YOUR GARDEN?

# Creating the look

With the practicalities and brief detour into feelings now covered, the next question for you to ask is what do you want the garden to look like? This is a big question and there are a few factors that are going to influence your answer.

## The architecture of your house

The architecture of your house is going to inform the aesthetic of your garden, whether you like it or not. Good design is about creating harmony. If you have a modern house, then a more contemporary scheme is going to sit better alongside it. Equally, if you have a lovely old farmhouse, you're going to need to lean more into the country feel (don't worry, you don't have to go full Beatrix Potter unless you want to). Now, please don't despair, it doesn't mean you can't bring in elements of what you love, it just means we need to be clever about it, with careful material choices and planting to make sure the garden feels like it belongs to the house, and vice versa.

## The style of your interiors

The style of your garden needs to reflect the style of your interiors. This is something I talk about all the time because it is an element of garden design that is so often overlooked in house and garden renovations. It is absolutely vital that the two are harmonious and that the spaces speak to each other. Why? Well, unless you live in a house with no windows (in which case, I have questions), your garden is very much connected to your house – each window acts as a frame for your garden. We'll get into focal points later on (see p50), but for now, we are talking about the style.

Now this doesn't mean you have to go all matchy-matchy with your materials, although this can be fabulous and we'll dive into it later (see p98), but it does mean that the two need to work in harmony. Just think how jarring it would be if you had an informal country farmhouse aesthetic inside, all squishy cushions and chintzy wallpapers, and outside you look onto a sea of minimalist grey paving and sculptural planting – it would look utterly bizarre.

The floor treatments on your ground floor, for example, particularly those that adjoin the outdoor terraces, are going to inform the colours of your paving, the style of your outdoor design, and possibly even the planting. I am not suggesting you match your cushions to your geraniums – now there's a thought – but design harmony from indoors to out is key.

The contemporary diagonal lines of the window frames on the house are echoed in the garden through the diagonal trellising and rear louvres. A modern and minimalist design reflects the interiors.

## Your climate and location

Like it or not, your climate is also going to impact the style of your garden. You might love the idea of an Italianate garden full of sun-loving plants, but if you live in a shady frost pocket where it rains nine months of the year, we might need to rethink the plan. We will be selecting plants that thrive in *your* garden – so we will be looking at soil type, aspect, wind, and region. More on this later (see pp134–35).

You also need to consider your location – not just in the world, but your surroundings. When designing gardens, I always research the history of the house and look up the typical materials of the area. Most of the time, the goal is to create a garden that feels harmonious with the surrounding landscape, not like it's been shipped in from a foreign land.

There is an expression that we designers love to use – the *genius loci*, which is a Latin term meaning the "spirit of a place". Essentially, it refers to the unique and often intangible qualities of a space, and the goal is to make sure that your garden reflects and complements the "spirit of the place", rather than jars with it. If you live in the rolling countryside, for example, then a more naturalistic feel is going to be appropriate for your garden. Anything too stark, urban, and contemporary is going to jar. The same is true with plant selection – the plants need to reflect the surrounding landscape, not least because we need to ensure that they thrive in the conditions. The goal for us, and now for you, is to try to respect the context of the site and work with it, not against it.

# Garden styles

There are plenty of styles to choose from when it comes to garden design, and I've outlined a few of the most common below. Use a moodboard (see pp24–25) to help you refine the style you like the most and that will work well in your garden.

## Traditional or formal gardens

Traditional gardens tend to feature symmetry and well-defined structure through the use of linear pathways, bold topiary, and plenty of formal hedging. Classic features include parterres, statues, and formal ponds, as well as well-manicured lawns (for croquet, of course). Just think of any stately home or National Trust property, and we're talking traditional.

## Cottage gardens

Cottage gardens tend to have a relaxed and romantic feel to them, categorized by an abundant mix of blowsy planting, herbs, and vegetables, and rustic features such as cobbles or old paving stones, mismatched furniture, and generally a much more naturalistic and informal feel.

WHAT DO YOU WANT FROM YOUR GARDEN?

## Japanese gardens

In Japanese-style gardens, the focus is on balance, simplicity, and harmony. The goal is a serene and meditative space, rich in symbolism. Typical features include rocks and boulders that are used to represent the natural landscape, along with gravel to denote rivers. Water features such as koi ponds or streams paired with bridges or platforms are also key features, along with acers, cherry blossom, and even bonsai.

## Modern and minimalist gardens

These gardens are uncluttered, sleek, and functional. They typically feature clean lines, with a restrained material palette consisting of stone, concrete, metal, or timber, usually in large format but not always. Planting tends to be an architectural detail in its own right, using clipped hedging, blocks of planting, and striking specimen trees. The colour palette is minimalist, usually with a focus on greens and whites.

## Modern country gardens

Modern country is a term best used to describe a mix of traditional and contemporary design elements. It usually features a more contemporary use of materials (think clean lines rather than rustic finishes) but with more naturalistic and soft planting. Planting tends to be grouped and soft, so rather than the informal chaos of cottage gardens or the rigid structure of minimalist gardens, it sits somewhere in between.

## Mediterranean gardens

These tend to have a rustic feel, though not always, and are inspired by the hot, dry Mediterranean climates of Italy, Spain, and Greece. Earthy tones are a feature, along with terracotta pots, drought-tolerant plants such as lavender, rosemary, and olive trees, lots of gravel, and maybe a water feature and colourful tiles.

## Tropical gardens

Tropical gardens are lush and verdant plant-filled spaces, with bold, exotic, large-leaved plants and bright flowers. Think immersive and jungly, with rich colours and a feeling of abundance.

## Wild gardens

These spaces are all about supporting wildlife, and have a wild and naturalistic style that attracts native creatures. Features include bird feeders, birdbaths, and ponds, bug or bee hotels, hedgehog boxes, pollinator-friendly planting, and plenty of shelter for insects and birds.

Dry-stone wall typical of the Cotswolds reflects the materials of the locality and is a nod to the area. A crisp Portland stone coping adds a contemporary twist to a traditional material.

Planting is abundant and romantic to contrast with the linear stone walls. Shades of purple pair beautifully with Cotswold stone.

WHAT DO YOU WANT FROM YOUR GARDEN?

A contemporary water rill guides the eye to the spectacular view beyond.

Different paving materials delineate journey spaces from seating areas. Smooth stone in the seating area matches the Portland coping on the walls, and cobbles are a nod to the heritage of the house, which was an old kennels and stables.

# DESIGNING A MOODBOARD

This one might seem obvious, but it's your garden, so you have to love it! First, you need to work out what your personal aesthetic is. So let's make a moodboard. Start by going on to Pinterest, Instagram, or Google, or go grab some garden magazines, and save/cut out shots of things you love. These ideas need to capture your garden as a whole, not just the plants, so be sure to include imagery of hardscape (your paving and pathways, for example) as well as plants, and all the other details from your wishlist such as pergolas, outdoor kitchen, and so on.

Lay all the images out together either on a computer or on a table. This is not only going to inspire you and get you excited about your garden, but also you will almost certainly notice a theme in what you love quickly emerging, which will help to focus the mind and keep you on a consistent design aesthetic. These choices are going to make up your moodboard of the garden. If you find your selection is a little chaotic, then edit it down to your absolute favourites and disregard the rest. Remember that restraint and consistency are key, and you need to stick to an aesthetic for your design to work well. I create a moodboard for every single garden I design, and it acts as a guiding light in design style and intent throughout the design process – so don't skip this step!

Take a look at your moodboard – does everything work together? Does anything jar or stick out? Does it feel harmonious with your house and interiors and true to your wishlist that we discussed earlier? Keep editing until you have a clear vision of the garden you want to achieve.

Your moodboard should include images that reflect the plants, colour palette, materials, shapes, and textures you love.

# THE PRACTICALITIES

Now that I've got you all excited thinking about your dream garden, we had better talk about some practicalities to make sure we can make it a reality. Budget, maintenance, and planning regulations are deeply boring things to consider, but vital, nonetheless.

## Your budget

Gulp. The money chat. There is a misconception that outdoor work is going to cost less than work on the house, and it's just not true. Chances are, unless you have a lovely little bijou courtyard (yum), your garden is larger than many of the rooms in your house. The fact is, building work costs the same whether it's indoors or out, so it's worth having a think about what you are willing to spend on your garden early on (see "How much should you spend?", below).

In terms of costs, the bigger your space, the easier it is for the costs to add up – it's a simple matter of scale. Hard landscaping (paving and so on) is almost always the priciest element, so keep an eye on the ever-growing wishlist and refine it down if need be. You could categorize your wishlist into the necessary, "nice to have", and aspirational.

The beauty of designing the garden as a whole now, even if it's out of budget to build all at once, is you can always revisit and build areas in future, which works far better than designing small sections that then don't work together as a cohesive whole. Once you have a design, you can always figure out which bits absolutely have to be installed immediately – such as the paving around the house – and what can wait a bit. And there are always ways to save, such as swapping materials for those that cost less or reusing materials, buying plants in smaller sizes or growing from seed, staggering the build, or doing some of the work yourself if you fancy some DIY.

### How much should you spend?

There's a general rule that spending about 10 to 15 per cent of the value of your home on the garden makes sense, as this is usually the amount of value you can expect to add to your house by doing the garden. This becomes moot if you plan to live there for 50 years and the value of the house is not of interest, rather than leaving in five years and hoping to make your money back.

WHAT DO YOU WANT FROM YOUR GARDEN?

Sometimes this 10 to 15 per cent rule is spot on, usually in urban and suburban spaces, but it's not something to cling to too tightly. If you live in a multi-million-pound townhouse in central London with a garden the size of a postage stamp, then it's unlikely you'll be spending 10–15 per cent of the value of your house on the garden (although not impossible – it all comes back to the wishlist). Equally, if you live in a very reasonably priced house but with acres of land, then chances are 10 per cent won't be enough to landscape the entire property. So the rule is flimsy, and I would much rather you ask yourself what you can afford and are willing to spend, and we'll go from there.

## Maintenance

You will need to maintain your garden. There is no such thing as a no-maintenance garden, and even low maintenance is still maintenance. Be honest with yourself about who is going to maintain it – yourself, someone in your household, or a paid professional. Even if you choose low-maintenance planting options, they aren't going to do the weeding for you, mow the lawn, or prune the shrubs, so be realistic with what you can commit to. This doesn't just extend to planting, either. Your hardscape needs maintenance just like the plants do, and there will be jet washing, sweeping, cleaning, and all sorts of other glamorous tasks to make sure the garden looks good year round. We'll cover material maintenance in Chapter 4, "Developing your design" (see pp66–101).

## Planning permissions and regulations

Green belt, areas of outstanding natural beauty, conservation areas, tree protection orders, agricultural land, estate committees, and many more regulated factors can impact the art of the possible. Be sure to do your homework on what is and isn't allowed where you live before you get too far with a design.

## What's next?

So, you should have now asked yourself how you want to use your garden, what features you want to include, who is using it, how you want it to look and feel, how long you plan to be there, and how much you can budget for the work. This, my dear friends, is your brief (see pp63–64 for some examples of garden briefs). Bravo – you are one step closer to designing your dream garden. Now that we have the client (your) brief down on paper, let's move on to the next step – understanding and surveying your garden.

2

# UNDERSTANDING YOUR GARDEN

SURVEYING THE SITE, SOIL, LIGHT, BOUNDARIES, AND SITE PLAN

The first step with all my designs is a site survey. This primarily involves measuring up the site so we can draw a design to scale, but it also looks at the site more holistically, noting down all the information that makes the garden unique – and now it's your turn. Think of it like taking a full inventory of your garden.

# SURVEYING THE SITE

Before you can start designing your garden, you need to understand the inner workings of it – namely, the soil, sunlight, local climate, and the size, as well as any weird and wonderful foibles. All gardens have foibles, whether it be a harsh wind, a noisy nearby road, a voracious tulip-eating deer colony, or neighbours who like a chat over the not-tall-enough fence (I can help with that). No two gardens are the same, and we need to design your garden with your specific space in mind.

## A bespoke design

I know it can be tempting to copy and paste a design from Pinterest, but trust me, it just won't work. That garden you are admiring will have been designed to work best for the conditions it finds itself in, and we need to do the same. It's a bit like when I realize I can't wear the same clothes as Hailey Bieber. It's a cruel fact that they just don't look the same on me – so it's better instead that I buy clothing that suits me. In much the same way, it's best we design your garden to suit your garden.

So, let's get to know your garden. The best way to do this is to watch it over a year so you can see how it behaves through the seasons, or even better, take photos. Perhaps you have been doing this already, or maybe its brand new to you – either way, start taking notice and make notes as the seasons change.

### The general vibe

This might sound a bit strange, but I need you to go outside and walk around your garden and notice the areas that you are drawn to. Make a note of the ones you naturally gravitate to and those you avoid. Which ones make you feel safe, calm, and peaceful? Which ones make you feel uneasy, stressed out, or just uncomfortable? Can you say why? Sometimes it's obvious – you feel overlooked by neighbours, there is an oppressive presence of overbearing trees, or it's just plain ugly. Sometimes it's not so obvious and there are just areas that feel calmer or more serene. I always walk around a new project to get a feel for the space – there will be areas I instinctively gravitate towards or avoid, and the same will be true for you.

## Listen for noise

When I visit a new garden, I always pause to listen. It's amazing how we learn to ignore the noises in our garden, so slow down and listen up – note down anything that you can hear, from road noise to aeroplanes or barking dogs. There isn't much we can do about the barking dogs, but we can introduce white noise for road sounds, or locate quieter spots in the garden as peaceful havens. Just note it down for now as it's all part of the survey of your garden.

## Look at the views

Next up, go and stand in your house and look out the windows. Just go with me here – go into the rooms you use the most, such as your kitchen, living room, office, or bedroom, and note down what your eye is led to. What do you see? This, my friend, is the current focal point(s) of your garden. Perhaps, like many with more urban spaces, your eye goes straight down the middle of the garden to the back fence (or the shed). Perhaps your eye darts all over the place with no obvious place to rest. You will be amazed how often the most frequented rooms in your house look onto the least attractive elements of a garden, such as a garden shed or trampoline. So note it down. We will be looking at focal points later (see p50) and they will inform the position of key elements.

## Climate

Climate is key when it comes to the design of your garden. In the UK and much of the rest of Europe and in the US, climate can vary from region to region. It's important we pay attention to this as we plan what you plant. Climate change is making this even more challenging, with previous garden staples proving vulnerable to the changing conditions, so be sure to pay attention to the typical temperatures and conditions of your area.

   Equally important is wind. Wind can savage a garden, so if you know your plot is vulnerable to wind, or perhaps you have a wind tunnel or two, note them down. Not only will we want to try to create a windbreak for you by perhaps installing some hedging, we also want to make sure the plants are resilient enough to take the buffeting.

This green gate was designed as a nod to the secret garden. The calming and classic colour complements the London stock bricks in the garden and the house. Rather than being a gate to anywhere, it in fact hides a storage space that was previously an awkward corner, and now acts as a wonderful focal point.

To mix up the materials in this small space, decking in a similar tone to the paving was installed as a pathway to the door. This delineates the seating area from the "journey" to the door, rather than allowing the space to blur into one.

UNDERSTANDING YOUR GARDEN

The sound of a bubbling water feature is wonderfully soothing, bringing an extra dimension to the garden that can muffle traffic noise. This terracotta water feature is positioned in direct view from the house, making it the perfect focal point not only in the garden but also from the house.

Adding a vertical structure, such as a trellis or pergola, creates more space for plants in a smaller garden and adds a feeling of enclosure and immersion. Use scented climbers, such as jasmine, to wrap your space in scent and provide perfumed seclusion as well as privacy.

# UNDERSTANDING SOIL

What type of soil your garden has is possibly the most important element that you need to grasp. When it comes to planting, knowing your soil is vital to understanding what you can and cannot plant, as different plants thrive in different conditions. There are two key factors we want to establish when analysing your soil – how acidic or alkaline it is and its structure.

## Acidic or alkaline?

The acidity or alkalinity of soil is measured by its pH level. Soil pH ranges from acid to alkaline on a scale of 1–14, with 0–6.5 being acidic (also known as ericaceous), 7 being neutral, and 7.5–14 being alkaline. Most soils range somewhere from pH 4.5 to 8.

You can get a fairly good idea of what pH your soil might be just by looking around you – if you have a garden stuffed full of rhododendrons, azaleas, and pines, you can bet good money your soil is acidic. Alternatively, if it's full of very happy lavender and lilacs, it may well be alkaline, but that's just giving you a hint. You need to be certain, and the way to do this is to buy an inexpensive soil pH

**ALKALINE SOILS**

Alkaline soils (pH 7.5–14) are rich in lime and typically sit on top of chalk or limestone. Plants such as lavender (right) and lilac grow best in alkaline soil.

**MODERATELY ACIDIC TO NEUTRAL SOILS**

Neutral soils (pH 6.5–7) allow for the widest range of plants to thrive as the nutrient availability is highest at this level. Roses, such as this *Rosa* BOSCOBEL ('Auscousin'), prefer well-drained neutral soil.

test online or in a garden centre. It is easy to do and involves nothing more than digging up a little soil and adding a small amount to a solution that changes colour based on the pH. On larger plots, you will need to test multiple areas, and it may be worth getting a soil test done by a specialist if the work you plan is extensive – it's money well spent.

## What soil pH is best?

The availability of nutrients in the soil varies based on the pH, so it depends what you want to grow. However, 6.5–7 is widely regarded as the optimum for most plants. You can check online for plants that prefer acid or alkaline soil.

## How do you know if a plant is happy in the pH?

When you buy a plant in the garden centre, the label will usually tell you what pH it needs, but if not, you can always look it up online. For those already in the ground, plants are pretty good at telling you if they aren't happy in their position. Signs that your plant is not loving the current pH include yellowing of the leaves, called chlorosis, as well as stunted growth, a failure to thrive, and curling leaves.

## Can I change the pH?

You can alter the pH of your soil, but this is an expensive and time-consuming process, so if you need to do this, limit it to the plants immediately by the house or specific plants. In large plots, it would be nearly impossible and it's far better to work with what you've got than fight it, which I would argue is true of most things in life. If you want to increase your soil pH, making it less acidic, then you can add lime (extremely carefully). Conversely, you can add acidifying materials such as sulphur chips or dust to decrease the soil pH.

**ACID SOILS**

Acid soils (pH 0–6.5) are often found in heathland and coniferous woodland areas, as decomposing plant matter acidifies the soil. Acid-loving plants include rhododendrons (right), azaleas, and camellias.

# Soil type

There are six different types of soil: sandy, loam, clay, silty, chalky, and peat. Much like the Seven Dwarfs, they each have distinct characteristics, and it's now time to get your hands dirty and figure out what you have with a little science experiment. Get a spade and dig a hole to a spade's depth and take the soil from the bottom (the top could just be new compost, mulch, or topsoil, which is why you need to go a bit deeper for it to be accurate). Now take a small scoop of the soil and add a little water – not too much, just enough to moisten it. See if you can roll the soil into a ball – add a little more water if need be. Now observe your soil.

- If you can't roll it into a ball and it crumbles in your hands *and* is gritty to the touch, then you have sandy soil.
- If you can roll it into a ball, now try rolling it into a sausage. If you can't do this, it may be you have a mix of sand and loam – also known as a sandy loam or loam.
- If you have an intact sausage (no sniggering), see if you can elongate it to a longer one. Is it smooth to the touch and can you smear it a bit? Is it a bit sticky? This is classic of clay. Just think of art lessons when you made a thumb pot.
- Silty soils are unusual, but if it doesn't clump easily, and is slippery and almost soapy in quality, you could be looking at silt.
- Chalky soils will usually have little lumps of chalk in them and are very alkaline.
- Peat soils are made mostly of organic matter. They are very fertile and hold lots of moisture, but are very rare in gardens.

# Soil compaction and rubble

If you have a new-build house, or have had building works done, then you may find the soil in your garden is compacted. Compaction is caused by heavy machinery, materials, or lots of footfall compressing the soil particles together, removing the air and preventing the movement of water through the soil. Your soil will feel rock solid, and you can tell it's compacted by the revolting smell that emerges when you start digging it! Plants will not thrive in a compacted soil as their roots will struggle to establish, not to mention it will likely pool water, so it's important to aerate it by forking or digging to loosen it up and potentially adding in some organic matter. If the soil compaction is really severe, this won't be enough, and you'll need the help of a good landscaping or lawn maintenance company to come and aerate the soil more deeply.

You may also find a lot of rubble in the ground, or a thin layer of topsoil spread over a rubbly or poor-condition soil. There's mixed opinions on the best approach here – purist gardeners would insist that you clear the borders of all rubble to give the plants the best chance, but a growing contingent of "resilient" gardeners are of the view we can work with it, as long as we choose the right plants. Just look at gardens such as Beth Chatto's or Knepp, which are growing on concrete or aggregate. So there are exceptions to the rule, and if in doubt, make sure your borders are rubble free.

# SOIL TYPES CHARACTERISTICS

### SAND

Sandy soils have a high proportion of – you guessed it – sand. This is a very light soil that makes it a dream to dig. It warms up quicker than clay but drains quickly after watering or rain, so it can become very dry in the summer and struggle to hold onto nutrients, which quickly wash away. You can improve sandy soils by adding plenty of organic matter, such as well-rotted manure or peat-free compost, to help retain both nutrients and moisture.

### PEAT

Peat soil is made up largely of organic matter and is usually quite acidic and very fertile. It holds a lot of moisture and is rarely found in gardens.

### CHALK

Chalky soils tend to be stony and free draining, are made up of a large amount of calcium carbonate, and are very alkaline.

### LOAM

Loam soils are arguably the gardener's dream. They are a mix of clay, silt, and sand and are a brilliant combination of fertile, free draining (but not too much), and easy to work with.

### SILT SOILS

Silty soils are more fertile and water retentive than sandy soil, but are still relatively free draining. They are easily compacted. You can improve silty soils by adding plenty of organic matter, which will help in retaining both nutrients and moisture.

### CLAY SOIL

Clay soil tends to be tricky to dig and drains poorly, instead holding onto water. It is slow to warm up in spring, and is known to crack in summer when it dries out. In winter, it can feel sticky and slimy. But it's not all awful – clay soil tends to be fertile as it holds onto nutrients and is good for water retention (which can be a pro and a con). As with sandy and silty soils, adding plenty of organic matter can greatly improve the soil structure.

Get to know the composition of your soil to help you understand which plants will thrive in your garden.

# ALL ABOUT LIGHT

I am obsessive about light. Light is one of the most crucial factors in any garden design. But that's not to say there is good light or bad light. Contrary to popular belief, I believe there are enormous merits to a north-facing garden – it's just about designing it properly.

## Understanding aspect

We need to understand the way light falls in the garden, or its aspect, for a couple of reasons. First of all, light determines the position of various elements in your garden, such as dining spaces and vegetable beds. Usually, I try to position a relaxed seating area for a morning coffee in an east-facing spot where the morning sun is. I might position a dining table either in shade or sun, depending on preference. And I will always look to add some kind of seating in a west-facing spot to enjoy the evening sun. Secondly, understanding sunlight in your garden is also going to tell you what plants will thrive in the various areas of your garden, as each plant has its own light requirements.

You can get a good idea of where the sun and shade might fall in your garden at various times of day by using the compass on your phone – the sun rises in the east and sets in the west, so you can predict where the sun will be throughout the day. Stand with your back to the house and see where the compass points. This is the aspect the garden is facing. There are also some handy apps that will show you how light moves in your garden, albeit they can't factor in the surrounds so well.

### Follow the sun

While a compass is going to give you a rough idea, it doesn't take into account neighbouring houses or trees that can greatly impact how much light your garden receives. So to really understand the light in the garden, the best thing you can do is watch it. Choose a day, preferably in summer, when you are at home all day. Set an alarm for each hour or so to remind you to look where the sun is, and check what parts of the garden are in sun and shade at various times in the day. Sketch out a rough shape of your garden and mark your observations at different times of day. Note down anywhere that seems to be permanently sunny or permanently in shade. Once you have this information, choosing where you position elements in the garden is going to be so much easier.

# GARDEN ASPECT

The direction your garden faces affects how much sunlight it receives and where. The aspect will influence where you place certain areas, such as a spot for morning coffee, and what plants will thrive in the light conditions.

## SOUTH FACING

The area by the house will be in sun for most of the day, with the opposite end of the garden in shade. If you like to sit in the sun, a space right outside the house will afford you the most sunshine, or on the left boundary for evening sun.

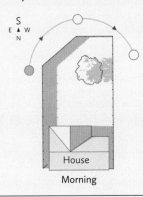

Morning

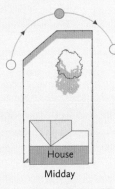

Midday

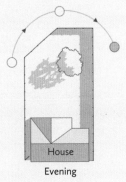

Evening

## NORTH FACING

The area by the house will be in shade for much of the day, making it great for a shady dining spot. Position seating areas for sun at the far end of the garden, or on the right boundary for late afternoon and evening sun.

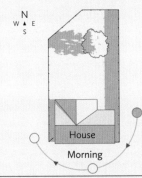

Morning

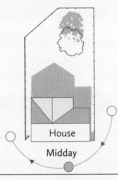

Midday

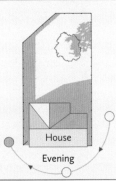

Evening

## EAST FACING

The area by the house will get morning sun, making it perfect for a morning coffee spot. By the afternoon, it will be in shade, so think about putting a seating space at the end of the garden for afternoon and evening sun, or on the left boundary for all-day sun.

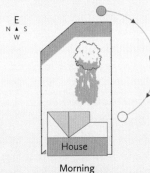

Morning

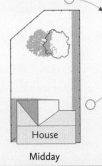

Midday

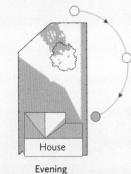

Evening

## WEST FACING

Position a morning coffee spot at the end of the garden, which will get the most sun. The area by the house will get sun all afternoon and evening, making it a fabulous aspect for sundowner cocktails and evening meals.

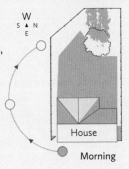

Morning

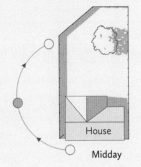

Midday

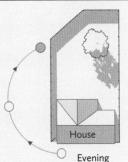

Evening

# BOUNDARIES AND NEIGHBOURS

We all need good boundaries – both in our lives and in our gardens. Boundaries can be a real point of contention, particularly when it comes to tired fences, crumbling walls, overbearing trees, or invasive weeds.

## Who owns the boundary?

It can be a bit of a mystery figuring out who owns what, and the days of the "bad side of the fence" rule are long gone. If you can, check your deeds or sale documents to see if you can find out what you do and don't own, and are therefore responsible for maintaining. If that doesn't work, you can always ask your neighbours, although their answers aren't necessarily reliable and may depend on who needs to shell out for repairs.

## Pruning boundary plants

There are a few nuances on boundary ownership that are worth knowing. Legally, you are permitted to cut off any part of a tree or plant that encroaches over your boundary. You can even climb into the tree to cut it – just as long as you don't trespass onto the nextdoor boundary and it doesn't have a tree protection order or is in a conservation area. You don't have to give notice for this, but if you want to keep things friendly, then it might be wise to. It's a myth that it's the owner's responsibility to dispose of the prunings and you can just dump them over the fence. In theory, you should offer the owner the prunings (I am fascinated to know if anyone ever takes them), and if they don't want them, dispose of them yourself. Do be careful if you prune a tree – killing it could be deemed negligent, so if in doubt, call a tree surgeon.

## Mending fences

You are responsible for repairing any fences you own. You may not own a fence that is on its last legs and be faced with the dilemma of a neighbour who doesn't wish to replace it. Here, you have a few choices: approach the neighbour and ask to split the cost, fund the thing yourself (not a popular choice but needs must), or install another fence or hedge within your boundary to mask their decrepit one.

Evergreen star jasmine (*Trachelospermum jasminoides*) twines between an ornate trellis to soften the boundary without overpowering it.

# How high?

When it comes to height, most garden fences are permitted up to a height of 2m (6½ft), and that includes a trellis on top, not in addition. Front garden fences and those adjoining a public highway are meant to be 1m (3ft). The exception to this is if you are replacing or repairing an existing structure. If you want a higher fence, you will need to get planning permission. Some boroughs or estates have specific rules on what you can and can't use, so do check.

As with all things in life, it's just worth being a decent human about these things, and it's amazing how far you can get just by being kind and considerate, so start with that. If all fails, you now know what you can and can't do.

## PAINTING THE FENCE

Fun fact: you aren't actually meant to paint or attach anything to a boundary that you don't own, so it's worth finding out which is yours to avoid any future aggro. If you do wish to paint it, ask first. If you own the fence, paint away – you own both sides of it – but again, it doesn't hurt to warn neighbours, it's just neighbourly.

# MEASURE YOUR GARDEN

Now we get into the real nitty gritty of it – measuring your garden. We want to do this so that we can map out the exact size and shape of it to scale, including existing features. You need this to make sure you can then design a garden that has accurate and practical proportions, else it's a bit like buying clothing without knowing your dress size – things just won't fit right.

Now, before I do this, I often like to hop onto Google Earth to take a look at the garden from above. You'll be amazed how often this shows that your rectangular garden is, in fact, more of a wonky triangle, has wobbly boundaries, or some other peccadillo. But that's just a starter for 10. We need to actually measure it.

## MEASURING UP

If you are measuring yourself, you are going to need a long tape measure – say, 30m (100ft) – as well as a shorter measure. I have had mixed success with inexpensive laser pointers too. Measuring is also going to be way easier with the help of someone else to hold the other end of the tape measure, or you are going to be running back and forth like a blue-arsed fly.

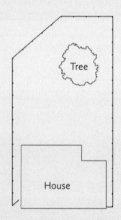

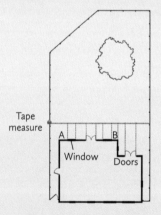

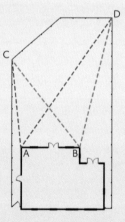

1. Take a piece of A3 or larger paper so you have space to scribble, and sketch out the rough shape of your garden and your house. It needn't be accurate – it's just so you can note down the measurements of each boundary and we'll get to drawing it to scale later (see pp44–45). Also sketch in any fixed elements such as big trees, structures, or walls.

2. You need an accurate measure of the back of your house (or the side that faces the garden) as this will be the baseline of your measurements. Measure from one end to the other, A to B. Lay the tape measure on the ground along the house and note down the measurements of doors, windows, drains, and any protruding sections, such as an extension. Take measurements of the other house sides.

3. Now, you are going to triangulate the space to capture the location of elements such as boundaries and any major features. Measure from the left house corner (A) to the left back boundary corner (C). Then measure to the right corner of the back boundary (D). Repeat from the right house corner (B). This gives you the location of the back boundary corners.

## Do you need a surveyor?

If you have a small garden, measuring is a pretty straightforward task. If, however, you have a larger space, or one with undulating levels or many twists and turns, then this starts to get rather tricky, and it may just be easier to call in a surveyor to do it for you. They will produce a topographic survey, which will show your entire garden to scale, including the levels, utilities, and locations of all key features, such as trees, shrubs, paving, pathways, and so on. I couldn't design a garden without it, so don't be a hero, and call in the experts if you are struggling.

It's common for topographical surveys to be conducted if you are having house works done, such as an extension, so be sure to ask them to survey the whole site, not just around the house. If you are really lucky and own the house, there might have been a survey left behind when you bought the house – it's worth checking.

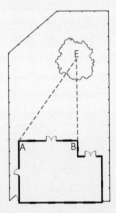

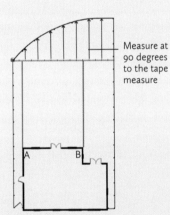

Measure at 90 degrees to the tape measure

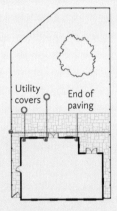

Utility covers

End of paving

4. Repeat this process for other, distant elements in your garden, such as a tree (E) or shed, continuing to use the two corners of the house (A and B) as the baseline. Each element should have three measurements: so for the tree (E), for instance, you have A–B, A–E, and B–E.

5. If you have curves in the garden, you can take offsets off a baseline at regular intervals. Measure two lines of the same length at right angles to the house at A and B. Lay a tape measure at right angles to them, parallel with the house. Measure at regular intervals along the line to the curve. Make a note of the measurements and the distance between the intervals.

6. Next, you can take some offset measurements of elements near the house, such as utility covers and the end of the paving. Run one tape measure along the back of the house (the house tape), and use another to measure at a right angle to certain features. You should note where on the house tape the feature is aligned and how far away from the house tape it is.

# DRAWING A SITE PLAN

So now we have the measurements of your garden, you need to draw it up to scale. It can be easier to do this on graph paper, but you can also do it on the computer if you have any computer-aided design (CAD) software. Let's have a look at how we do this with graph paper.

## Working to scale

The scale that's going to work for your garden depends on its size. Most work well with 1:50, where 1cm represents 50cm, but you might need to go up to 1:100 (1cm is 100cm or 1m) or 1:200 (1cm is 200cm or 2m) for larger plots.

First, measure the longest length in your garden. This is going to tell you what scale is going to work for you in terms of actually fitting your design on paper. I like to use A3 graph paper so I have enough space, but if you have a big garden, you might need to size up to A2 to avoid going to the rather hefty scale of 1:500.

Let's say your longest measurement is 20m. This is going to equate to 20cm on a 1:100 scale or 40cm on 1:50. So you need a piece of paper that can easily accommodate 20cm or 40cm as your largest measurement – *capiche*?

To draw up your plan, you need a ruler or, even better, a scale ruler (which are cheap to buy and worth investing in) and a compass, which is 100 per cent going to take you right back to maths class. Shudder.

# Plotting the boundaries

Let's work an example at 1:50 to plot your boundaries and other elements to scale. You may find that you need to increase or decrease the scale you use to get it to a comfortable size to design with – you don't want anything too small and fiddly – so experiment.

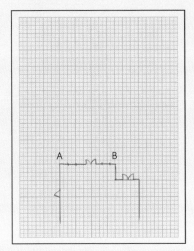

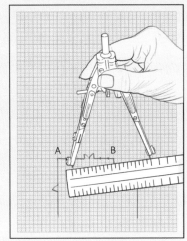

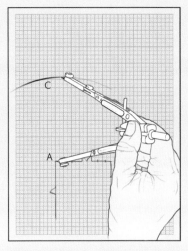

1. Your house is 7m wide (A–B). Draw a 14cm line towards the bottom of your paper. You have a door at 3m along, which is 1m wide. Mark the position of the door at 6–8cm. Repeat for the other elements on the house, such as windows, that you measured before.

2. Take your compass and position it at the scaled amount for A–C (left house corner to the left back boundary corner) that you measured before. Let's say it's 10m away from the left corner of the house, so set the compass to 20cm.

3. Position the pointy end of the compass on point A and then do a little sweep in the general direction of the left back boundary corner (C). Now set your compass for the scaled amount of B–C (right house corner to the left back boundary corner). Let's say it's 13m, so set the compass to 26cm.

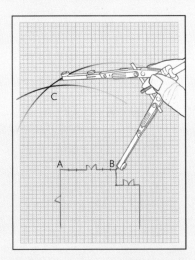

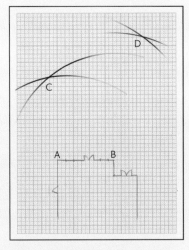

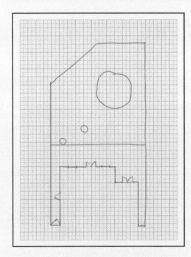

4. Position the point of the compass on point B and then do another little sweep in the general direction of the left back boundary corner (C). Something magic will happen. The two points will cross over, and ta-da – you have the location of your left back boundary corner!

5. Now repeat this for the other corner (D), doing compass sweeps from A to D and from B to D. Repeat the process for any angles in your boundary, and for all the noted elements in your garden, such as utility covers and trees.

6. Join all the boundary points together and erase the compass sweeps. Mark the location of the other elements. And then, oh my goodness, we have a scaled drawing of your garden, *you absolute hero.*

# A note on levels

Flat gardens are rare. Even if you think your garden is flat, I'd bet good money it isn't. Squat down and look at the topography of your garden – notice if there are any slight slopes or variations. If your garden is very clearly on a massive slope, I shall spare you the squatting.

You can also gain information on levels by measuring the heights of steps and walls in your garden. For more complex levels, you can hire a laser level. Or you can get all of this information from a topographical survey (see p43), which is really worth doing if you have anything beyond fairly gentle slopes.

## MEASURING A SLOPE

Now we get to the business of measuring the levels, and for this you need a tape measure, string, two wooden pegs or bamboo canes, a hammer or mallet, and a spirit level.

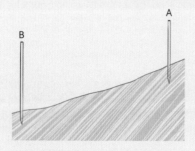

1. On gentle slopes, hammer two pegs or canes into the ground: one at the top of the slope (A) and one at the bottom (B). The bottom peg or cane will need to be tall enough to accommodate the height of the slope.

2. Attach the string at the very bottom of the top peg (A). Then take the string down the slope until you reach the bottom. Tie the string around the bottom peg or cane (B) so it's level with the top peg – use a spirit level to help.

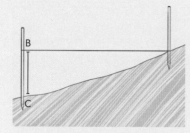

3. Then measure the distance from the string height on the bottom peg (B) to the ground (C). This is going to give you the height of your slope, and then you can work out how many steps or terraces you're going to need (see pp57–58).

UNDERSTANDING YOUR GARDEN

This garden was previously
on a slope of around a metre
(3ft). To make the garden
more useable, the terrace was
levelled and steps introduced
down to the lower lawn level.

DRAWING A SITE PLAN

3

# DESIGNING YOUR GARDEN

DESIGN PRINCIPLES, ZONING PLAN, THE GRID, SCALE
AND LEVELS, AND THE CONCEPT PLAN

You have a full survey of your garden and a wishlist to
hand. You know what you want it to look like and you've
got to know the inner workings of your space, from soil to
sunlight. Now comes the fun part. We are going to take all the
information and translate it into a design that works just for you.

# DESIGN PRINCIPLES

In this chapter, we're going to create your concept plan, which is a
general idea of the garden in terms of how the space flows. As well
as the garden layout, it will be informed by a zoning plan and a scaled
grid of your space so you can calculate dimensions and also materials.

First of all, though, I'm going to talk you through some basic design principles
that you can keep in mind when looking at your garden design:

**Balance** This is the ultimate aim of your design. We want the garden to feel like
it is balanced in terms of proportions and the ratio of the mass to the void. The
mass is planting, furniture, or structures, and the void is flat surfaces, such as lawn,
paving, and pathways. As a general rule, we want about 60 per cent of your garden
to be planting (mass), and 40 per cent to be paved/lawn (void). This is usually
where most people trip up and go too far in the other direction – lots of paving,
not enough plants.

**Emphasis/focal points** We want the eye to go to the right places in the garden.
Whether that be straight to one key piece, sliding across the garden, or bouncing
between several key features is up to you. Views from your house are crucial in
considering placement of key features, so take note of your focal points.

**Harmonious design** The garden needs to feel like an extension of your home.
This doesn't have to mean a literal match in materiality or colours, but the design
language has to be harmonious with the architecture of the house, the interior
décor, and the wider environment.

**Repetition** Good design often sees the repetition of elements, whether it be a
material, a pattern, a shape, or a colour, to provide rhythm and cohesion. This is
true of both materials and planting (see pp100 and 140–41 for more detail).

These repeating arches not
only add a sense of journey,
but also balance out a large
wall on the opposite side of
the garden, bringing height
and harmony to the space.

**Practicality and function** This one is easy to overlook, but it's the difference
between a pretty garden and a pretty *and* useable garden. At the heart of the
design must be your intended use – this is where your wishlist comes in handy.

Adding a curve to a path can instantly create interest and eliminate the risk of tunnel vision.

**Avoid tunnel vision.** This one's going to take a little convincing, but a good design is often one that you can't see all at once. We want to have drama, interest, and surprise in a garden. Exploration is the name of the game, and you can't explore something you can see all at once. Aim for a design where your eye isn't going directly to the back of the plot without any interruption. This interruption doesn't have to be a solid visual block, such as a tall hedge or wall, but it should be something that brings interest into the foreground. It could be planting that you look through, a lovely tree, a low hedge, or a pathway that crosses the space.

**Nature is very rarely symmetrical and symmetry is rarely the answer.** This one was hard to swallow when I was studying, and I suspect it will be for you too. The best designs are usually those that – gulp – aren't symmetrical. Now, these rules

DESIGNING YOUR GARDEN

don't apply if we are going terribly formal – in that case, symmetry works – but usually, we try to avoid it. Trust me, you can create a balanced design without it being matchy-matchy on both sides.

**Pathways don't have to be straight lines to their destination.** This is an odd one, but I like my pathways to change direction, or if they don't, I like to be sure there is something to look at at the end of the pathway, such as a beautiful tree, pot, sculpture, or bench. It's fine for a path to wind or to lead you in one direction then another – this creates prettier views and interest.

**Conceal the ugly bits.** When young humans are tiny, they need supervising, so yes, play equipment needs to be where you can keep an eye on them. But as they grow up, you don't need to supervise so much, so keep that in mind when choosing the all-important location of the trampoline. You can always plant a hedge in future. Likewise sheds – no one needs one as a focal point, so remember to put something in front to obscure the view, or even better, avoid putting it in key sightlines.

**You need a journey and a destination.** A mantra for life and one for your garden – you need to actually have a reason to go *into* the garden, and that is much more inviting if you have somewhere to go and a means of getting there. If you have to cross a lawn to get to it, you're less likely to use it – and so we have pathways.

**Mix up the journey.** If possible, I want your garden to flow but not in a straight line. This is easier in a large garden than in a small one, but it means you avoid the tunnel vision mentioned above, and add a bit of "journey" to your garden. Think of it this way: if you enter a space at one point, then avoid having the exit in line with the entry point. Send yourself in a different direction – it's more interesting.

**Don't forget height.** Height can really bring interest to a garden, so consider if you want to include a pergola, some archways, parasol trees, and so on.

**Get into the garden!** Try to avoid putting all seating options by the house, and instead, introduce at least one seating space within the garden that invites you to actually be in the garden, rather than sitting by the house just looking at it.

**Don't be scared of levels.** Changing the levels in the garden, even by one or two steps, instantly adds interest to a space. If you have a sloping garden, it's a great opportunity to lean into this and instantly add different rooms to the garden.

**Delineate front and back gardens.** Many houses sit within a plot where the garden wraps around the house. My first priority is delineating the front and back garden into two separate spaces with hedging, gates, fences, or walls. This not only adds the benefit of extra security, but dividing the front and back garden creates a greater sense of enclosure.

# THE ZONING PLAN

Before we get into the nitty gritty of the design, we are going to start with a zoning plan. This does what it says on the tin – we are going to figure out your zones or, in other words, where everything is going to go.

## Start with tracing paper

When I design, I always start on tracing paper. You overlay this over your lovely new, drawn-to-scale site plan. It means you aren't constantly redrawing the plan perfectly, but just overlaying a new sheet of tracing paper if things go pear shaped or you want to try other ideas. Your site plan should be seen as the masterplan – don't draw on it ever. That way, you need only draw it perfectly once!

So let's get started. Take your very first piece of tracing paper – how exciting – and lay it over your site plan. In design school, we were taught to tape the corners of both down with masking tape – that's

up to you, but it can help keep it all neatly overlaid. Then trace over the outline of your garden – it really needn't be perfect but it's just to show you the boundaries of the garden. This is the first step every time you start a new design for the space – draw the outline so you know what you're dealing with. Then mark in anything that is staying in the garden (existing trees and so on) as well as the key doors and windows on your house that overlook the garden.

## Mark the zones

All you are going to do is mark on the plan where you want the largest things from your wishlist to be. Keep this to the big elements such as the dining area, play space, or veg garden, but don't worry about the little bits like the washing line. So, for example, if your wishlist is a dining terrace, a greenhouse, and a spot for morning coffee, just draw a circle and label it. Here's an example of mine (left).

Now, the trick with your zoning plan is to remember to factor in sunlight, surroundings, and views from the house. So play around with it, checking that your seating areas are in sun/shade when you want them to be, that you haven't accidentally placed a climbing frame as your focal point from your most-used window of the house, and that you haven't placed sunloungers in deep shade (unless you want to). Refer back to your notes on how you want your garden to feel, how you felt in certain areas, and how you want to use those areas.

# THE GRID

So you've got the zoning plan and you're largely happy with the rough locations of things. Now I am going to introduce you to the grid. This is a popular method taught by some design schools to help you figure out an interesting garden layout.

It allows you to have a good play around with shapes and patterns, make sure that the areas of your garden are nicely aligned with the house and your key views from within, and helps to create a garden with good mass (planting and structures) and void (lawn and paths) ratios. The beauty of this system is that it's going to allow you to design at a reasonable scale from the get-go, as well as ensuring sightlines are well aligned to your house from the very beginning.

## Drawing the grid

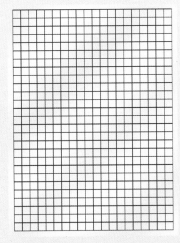

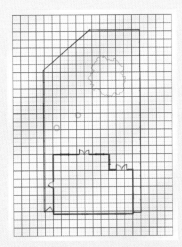

1. Take a piece of tracing paper and put a piece of graph paper underneath so that you have some lines to follow (or you can use a set square if you have one). Now, measure 1m on your scale rule (the scale you used for your site plan), and draw a grid on your tracing paper in which each square represents 1sq m (if your garden is vast, you could do 2sq m). The graph paper will help you follow the lines, but do use a ruler, obvs. The point of this exercise is so you can draw your garden with rough dimensions in mind.

2. Lay your tracing-paper grid on top of your site plan. Then overlay another piece of tracing paper on top of this (never draw on your grid), do a quick trace of the boundaries, windows, and doors so you can see the shape of the garden and key views and access points. Align your grid with a corner of your house – don't worry if it doesn't fit the house neatly, just choose an important corner and align it. This is a great trick as it will instantly show you the focal points from each of your windows and doors, making it easier to position things either in, or out of, those key views.

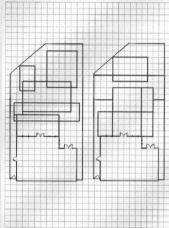
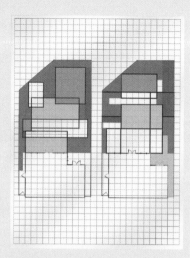
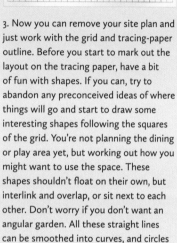

3. Now you can remove your site plan and just work with the grid and tracing-paper outline. Before you start to mark out the layout on the tracing paper, have a bit of fun with shapes. If you can, try to abandon any preconceived ideas of where things will go and start to draw some interesting shapes following the squares of the grid. You're not planning the dining or play area yet, but working out how you might want to use the space. These shapes shouldn't float on their own, but interlink and overlap, or sit next to each other. Don't worry if you don't want an angular garden. All these straight lines can be smoothed into curves, and circles can be added later.

4. Once you've filled the garden with shapes, start to colour or shade a few in. You could fill in the whole shape, or just the area that isn't overlapped. The key word at this stage is *play*, so play around. It's inevitable your mind will be deciding what is what (lawn and so on), probably based on what you already have in mind for the garden, but if you can, just have some fun scribbling in some of the boxes in your pattern and leaving others. If you want to be more pragmatic and less artsy, you can just follow the grid to create the layout you want, but you will be surprised what might come up for you with the creative scribbles first, so indulge me.

Now do another one that is totally different. We were always taught to do multiple – so force yourself to try different arrangements, even if they aren't what you want. Just experiment and produce three, four, or even 10 if you want.

You can also turn the grid to be at a different angle. This can work very well in narrow spaces or odd-shaped gardens where straight lines from the house don't feel right. I do this far less often, as I try wherever possible to avoid creating triangles, which create awkward and unintentional focal points that designing on an angle can bring about.

Hopefully, by now you have created some interesting shapes and patterns, and maybe you can already see how this might relate to your finished garden layout. Now you can take these patterns and shapes and translate them into a practical and flowing layout that works well. Your grid has likely allowed you to create a layout with sensible sizes for each of your elements, but let's take a closer look at scale.

# LOOKING AT SCALE

As a general rule, you need to be more generous with your spacing outdoors than in, so don't try to design your garden based on interior dimensions. Pathways, seating areas, and even steps tend to be on a larger scale outdoors. If you want to really geek out, and I suggest you do, go and grab a tape measure and measure a few elements of your or your friends' garden, or, even better, public spaces.

I have had some very strange looks as a result of doing this – most notably at the RHS garden at Wisley, where I was forensically measuring a particularly lovely set of steps. Understanding the comfortable height of a step, or the useable width of a path, is going to make your garden work so much better than guesswork.

## Pathways and access

Let's get into a little more detail on some typical dimensions so you can be sure you are getting the layout right. Usually, we aim for pathways to be a generous width, commonly around 100–160cm (3–5ft) wide. The larger end of this allows two people to walk side by side in a garden. Of course, a very wide path would feel disproportionate in a small garden, and this is where your grid will quickly show you what will and won't work for the space. In smaller spaces, or where we are doing a more informal cut-through or utility path, we would reduce the width to around 60–80cm (24–32in) at a push. For wheelchair-accessible routes, be sure to make pathways a minimum of 120cm (4ft).

Don't forget to consider access for lawnmowers, wheelbarrows, bikes, and anything else you might want to manoeuvre around the garden. In larger spaces that might need some substantial tree surgery or use of a ride-on mower, it's vital you leave enough access for machinery to get into and around the garden.

## Steps and ramps

Steps outdoors need to be deeper, wider, and less steep than interior stairs, so totally ignore what you would do inside. If you followed those rules, the steps would be anywhere from uncomfortable to downright dangerous. A standard measurement I aspire to is a riser of around 150–180mm (6–7in) and a tread of no less than 300mm (12in), but preferably closer to 400mm (16in) or more. Much of this will be determined by your chosen material, but more on that later (see Chapter 4). Be sure to avoid risers that are smaller than 150mm (6in) – they are essentially a trip hazard – and more than 200mm (8in) becomes quite the effort.

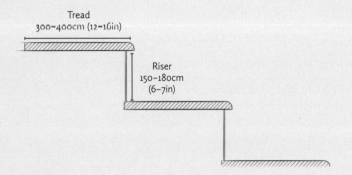

Tread
300–400cm (12–16in)

Riser
150–180cm
(6–7in)

Treads should ideally be a minimum of 300cm (12in) and risers 150cm (6in). Make sure all steps are the same height and depth to avoid creating a trip hazard.

One cardinal rule is your steps must be equal and all have the same riser height and tread depth, or else trips are inevitable. If you have a very long run of steps, it's advisable to introduce a platform for pausing.

Ramps are a great alternative to steps and allow your garden to be accessible for all. They should have a minimum gradient of 1:12, but 1:15 or 1:20 is more manageable, and, like pathways, have a minimum width of 120cm (4ft).

## Dining areas

Dining areas are arguably the easiest to get wrong, so the grid comes in handy here. As a general rule, you want an absolute minimum of 80–100cm (32–39in) around any furniture to ensure you can get past it without banging into it. Then you need to allow enough space for your furniture and the practicalities of use, such as pushing a chair out from the table.

A typical table is around 1m (3ft) wide, and a chair around 50cm (20in), which you need to be able to comfortably push out from the table and navigate around. Add 1m (3ft) for this and we are looking at 3.5–4m (11½–13ft), which is the minimum depth I would normally allow for a dining space.

While it can feel comforting to go the other way and hand over loads of space to the dining area, I would discourage this, as too much paving can feel sterile and cold. The best thing to do is figure out what size of furniture you want based on how many people you wish to seat, gather the dimensions of the table and chairs, and ensure you are adding enough space to negotiate around the table (with chairs in and out). Usually, unless you have a very large table, it falls between 4–6m by 4–6m (13–20ft). If you make it much larger without a break for some planting, the furniture can get lost in the space. To be absolutely certain, use marking-out spray paint or bamboo canes to mark it out and check it feels right, along with the intended furniture.

## Paving by the house

Usually, there will be hardscape immediately outside your back door. It may or may not constitute a dining or seating terrace, which will dictate how deep it needs to be. For dining or seating, follow the guidelines above and remember to also include journey space. If it's solely going to act as a transition into the garden, with no furniture, two strides tends to be a comfortable balance. Try to avoid the dreaded no-man's-land of 2–3m (6½–10ft), which is neither one thing nor t'other. Remember – use is key.

## Planting areas

This is going to be my toughest sell to you, but you cannot have puny borders if you want your garden to look good. Borders are what we designers call planting areas, also known as flowerbeds. If you want to absolutely ruin your design, you're going to add in a load of 60cm (2ft) wide borders and have a sad single row of plants in your garden. (I can barely write it – please don't do it.)

As a very general rule, I try to avoid any borders under 1m (3ft), but I would much rather your minimum (yes, minimum!) was closer to 1.2–1.5m (4–5ft) to allow you to actually have some depth in your planting. If you have a very compact space, I may be asking a lot of you, and 80cm (32in) is doable in such cases – we have to work with what we've got. But if you have anything above a very compact town garden, you have zero excuse and this is a hill I am willing to die on. "Can we reduce the planting down to allow for more lawn?" is a surefire way to crush my spirits and epically compromise a scheme.

Now this isn't me just being a sassy plant enthusiast – it's the fact that balance is key. You simply cannot have a garden which is 85 per cent paved and lawn and 15 per cent planting and expect it to look right. It would be the interior equivalent of having a room with just a sofa in it. Besides that being very bizarre, it's not inviting, immersive, or balanced. We can look at the lowest-maintenance plants of all time if that's the concern, but *lean into the plants* and give space to them – your garden will look better for it.

The deeper the border, the more interest you can add in the planting through height and seasonal variety.

# LOOKING AT LEVELS

If you have a sloping garden, it can be daunting figuring out how to design it to make it work for you. My typical aim with a sloped garden is to terrace at least some of it to give you some flat, useable space. Slopes by their nature do not allow for much use. This doesn't mean you must terrace the entire garden, nor does it mean you need to introduce copious costly retaining walls (though you might need to if you want to maximize the space).

Rather than seeing a slope as a bad thing, a sloping garden is a great opportunity to add interest and different "rooms" in a garden. In fact, it's often my aim with a flat garden to add some level changes for exactly that reason. Just remember – if you raise a level higher than 30cm (12in), you will probably need planning permission. Don't forget to consider water runoff from any slopes and factor in drainage to capture it.

If you have a gently sloping site, you can consider terracing spaces and having low-level retaining walls to keep the soil in place, or if space allows, ramping earth to create gentle slopes that can be either turfed or planted (do consider the maintenance of mowing) is a great and cost-saving solution.

On steeper slopes, you can have fun with landforms, where rather than a typical slope, you have tiered layers (think amphitheatre), which add a sense of play to a space. Where the slopes are more aggressive, or space is tighter, then retaining walls are inevitable to prevent soil tumbling down the slope. These are costly and will require the expertise of a structural engineer, and it's vital they include drainage behind the walls too.

## TOP TIP

If you have dramatic level changes, resist the urge to simply install one monolithic wall to create two different levels. This only serves to separate you completely from your garden, and can create a real eyesore in the garden when looking back at the house. Instead, try to divide the different levels into three so that you have a series of spaces, with gentle journeys up or down the slope. This eliminates the feeling of a cliff edge and huge expanses of wall – it's so much friendlier and allows for a better connection between house and garden as a whole. If you do find you have a large wall to contend with, then adding a raised planter in front can soften the effect.

## SAFETY FIRST

If you are creating level changes, it's vital you remember to include balustrades for any drops over 60cm (2ft).

Introducing several terraced levels in a sloping garden instantly makes it more useable.

# THE CONCEPT PLAN

You know your garden's aspect and where the main sightlines are, and have a zoning plan, patterns and shapes from your grid, and an idea of reasonable scale for various areas. Now you can translate this into a layout, or probably several layouts, of your space. Don't worry about materials yet – we'll get to it (see Chapter 4). This is what I call the concept plan, and all we are interested in is the layout and the flow of space. At the end of it, you should have something that looks like these examples.

Let's work through an example together.

## Worked example: urban garden

Your typical urban or suburban garden is usually some kind of long rectangle, and the trick with these is to cut across the garden to give the feeling of width and depth. Clients usually heavily resist at first because many have a strong affection for lawn and a desire to keep as much of it as possible, which makes for rather limited design options.

If you have small kids and want to maximize play space for them, there are two brutal truths to choose from. Either shelve the garden design until they are

older, cherish the madness and chaos of having tiny ones, and save the gorgeous garden until they are older. Or (and I feel a bit harsh saying this) accept that they will have less lawn to play on and you will have a fabulous-looking garden that you can all enjoy. You can't have it all unless you have the luxury of space, and so a decision must be made.

I'm going to imagine two worked examples here: one with a lawn and one without, so you can see the art of the possible.

The garden's aspect, zoning plan, key sightlines, and patterns from the grid all provide useful information to create different concept plans.

Aspect

Zoning plan

Key sightlines

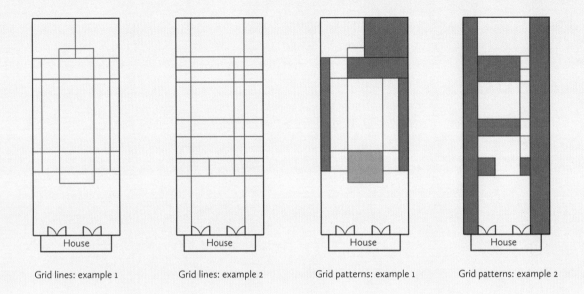

Grid lines: example 1    Grid lines: example 2    Grid patterns: example 1    Grid patterns: example 2

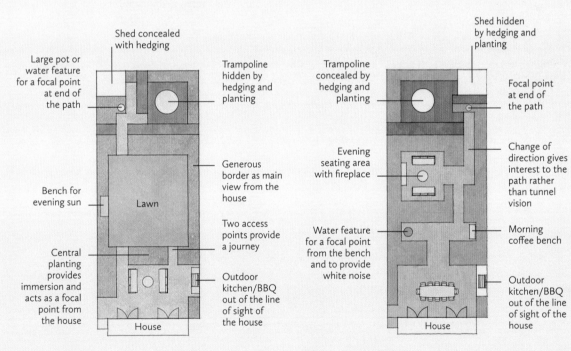

Shed concealed with hedging

Large pot or water feature for a focal point at end of the path

Trampoline hidden by hedging and planting

Generous border as main view from the house

Bench for evening sun

Lawn

Two access points provide a journey

Central planting provides immersion and acts as a focal point from the house

Outdoor kitchen/BBQ out of the line of sight of the house

House

**Brief 1:** Lawn, trampoline, shed, dining area, seating area, outdoor kitchen, plants
**Aspect:** South facing

Shed hidden by hedging and planting

Trampoline concealed by hedging and planting

Focal point at end of the path

Evening seating area with fireplace

Change of direction gives interest to the path rather than tunnel vision

Water feature for a focal point from the bench and to provide white noise

Morning coffee bench

Outdoor kitchen/BBQ out of the line of sight of the house

House

**Brief 2:** Trampoline, shed, dining area, seating area, plenty of plants, outdoor kitchen, no lawn
**Aspect:** South facing

# Large gardens

Large gardens scare a lot of people, as they look at the space in its entirety and wonder where to start, but really the reasoning is just the same as smaller spaces – the main focus of the design is what is happening around the house and close by. If you have acres of land, you certainly aren't going to hard landscape the whole thing. In fact, the general rule is that the most "designed" part of the garden is nearest the house. We then ease the house into the landscape by gently transitioning to less and less formal design as we move further away from the house. With large gardens, the goal is usually to divide the space into useable rooms or zones. In an urban garden, you might have one or two rooms, whereas in a larger garden, you can have more.

**Brief:** Lawn, seating areas, dining area, play area, water feature, and optional swimming pool
**Aspect:** Southeast facing

Sinuous path around the trampoline

Lawn

Pool

House

Vegetable garden with water feature

Topiary domes add interest to the lawn in this formal design

Seating area

Lawn

House

Pathways around the house create different journeys, dividing the garden into separate rooms

Water feature

Hidden trampoline

In larger gardens, focus on having the more formal elements close to the house, and allow for more planting and a looser feel as you move further away. Consider the aspect for clues on where to position things.

## THE TRICK WITH TRIANGLES

Often, you will find your garden is not, in fact, a neat rectangle or square, but actually has angles and awkward triangles in the space. Triangles and corners have a funny way of leading the eye into the apex of the triangle, making them an accidental focal point, so the first thing I do with any design is hide the triangles. You can do this by squaring or curving them off with planting, hedging, or anything that's going to obscure the corner of doom.

## Courtyard garden

This is one of my favourite styles of garden to design. No lawn and not enough space to get overcomplicated. Instead, the challenge with a courtyard garden is being restrained, and accepting that a courtyard must do one thing really well, rather than attempting to fit too much in. In courtyards, one of the best pieces of advice I can give you is to go oversized on your elements. Using lots of little elements only serves to make the space feel smaller than it is.

So the first thing to decide is use. Is it for eating and cooking, or sitting and relaxing, or pure garden immersion? Let's say in this instance the choice is for laid-back relaxation. This is often what I recommend in courtyard spaces that adjoin a kitchen, as usually there is a dining table close by. It all seems a bit pointless to put another one right next to it, when you can have some more comfortable sofas that can be used throughout the day and evening, making it more multifunctional.

**Brief:** Seating space and plenty of planting
**Aspect:** West facing

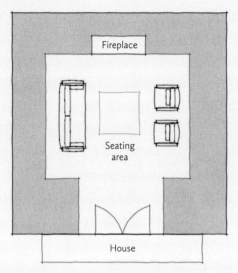

Generous borders surround the seating area, which enjoys afternoon and evening sun, and provide immersion. The fireplace at the end of the garden acts as a focal point.

## Roof terraces and balconies

Roof terraces and balconies are a tricky beast. They are exposed, there are weight limits to consider, and access is inevitably a challenge. I once designed a garden in central London where the only means of access was up very narrow, winding staircases. It made getting pots, soil, and plants up and through the house a logistical challenge to say the least.

The first thing to establish is whether your roof terrace can actually be used as a garden/leisure space – simply because an area is flat doesn't mean it has been designed to be weight bearing. So do check this before with a structural engineer as well as with your local council or a planning consultant to be sure there aren't any restrictions in place. It's worth contacting a structural engineer regardless, as understanding the weight limits of your roof terrace is absolutely vital. You cannot cut corners on this – wet soil, trees, furniture, and people are heavy, and making sure you are keeping well on the safe side of the limits is crucial.

Unless they are large enough to have more than one room/zone, most roof terraces and balconies have a similar principle to courtyards – you need to choose the use wisely. I like roof terraces to feel like a green oasis in the sky, with seating surrounded by planting at varying heights to make you feel fully immersed. This is great for pollinators as well as for you. If you are lucky enough to have a spectacular view, it's a no-brainer to orient the furniture to enjoy it to maximum effect. You may need to install paving on a pedestal system for drainage and weight reasons, or decking is also a popular option.

I don't use the same growing medium for roof terraces as on the ground – the aim is to lighten the load as much as possible. So you want to specify a roof terrace mix that usually contains compost and/or loam and some kind of lightweight substrate such as coir or lightweight expanded clay aggregate (LECA). We'll look at the perfect plants for a roof terrace or balcony on p147.

4

# DEVELOPING YOUR DESIGN

## HARDSCAPING, WHAT TO USE WHERE, SUSTAINABILITY, AND TIPS ON CHOOSING MATERIALS

At this point, you should have a good idea of how you want the space in your garden to flow. So now it's time to look at the materials that are available for your hardscaping and where best to use them. We'll also consider the importance of making sustainable and environmentally sensitive choices when developing your design.

# HARDSCAPING

Hardscaping refers to the ground works in your garden, such as paving, pathways, and walls. When I travel, I spend an inordinate amount of time admiring the ground – more specifically, the paving, but also walling, steps, and just about anything that involves some level of landscape design. My camera roll at the end of a holiday will be as much filled with cobbles and benches as it will be with happy memories with the kids.

The thing about studying design is it opens your eyes to a world that has always been there, you just haven't noticed it before. Try it yourself – next time you are out and about, notice the materials you are walking on. Have you noticed the chunky York stone paving in central London? Can you see the huge variety of patterns in the brick walls you pass? When you start looking, you start noticing.

One of the most bizarre parts of designing your own garden is that you are going to start noticing things you will quite literally not have thought twice about before. You're going to start seeing brick patterns, grout gaps, interesting gates – you name it. Frankly, the day you are stopped in your tracks by a particularly striking wall is the day you know you have been infected by the design bug, for which there is no known cure.

And so, without further ado, it's time to start picking out materials. Your choice of materials is going to be dictated by the factors we explored earlier in Chapter 1, including your house architecture and interiors, your moodboard aesthetic, and your surroundings and location.

## Gravel

I love gravel. In the studio, we have jars of the stuff and get very excited about it. It can be made of any number of rocks, from granite and limestone to sandstone, quartz, and flint, among others.

It's permeable, hard wearing, and inexpensive. The key is getting the size right for the use. As a general guide, for driveways you want to use a 20mm (¾in) size so you aren't tracking it into the house with your shoes or collecting it in your tyres. We tend to use a stabilization grid, which resembles a giant honeycomb sheet in which the gravel sits to avoid it migrating and feeling like you are driving on a beach. For pathways, 10–14mm (½–⅝in) is a good size. You can also use a smaller size – 6mm (¼in) to basically dust – which can be described as self-binding gravel and is what is used at public spaces such as National Trust properties. It's firm and hard wearing, although the dust can be a nuisance.

# Types of paving

So, what are your choices for large- and small-format paving? Let's start with large-format paving, which you will most likely want to use for paving close to the house, and for any other dining and seating areas, although you can mix it up with some smaller-format pavers too – we'll get to that next (see pp74–76). One of the best things you can do is visit a paving showroom, preferably one that is a specialist in outdoor paving rather than an interior showroom with a few exterior choices. Check out the list of suppliers on p186.

When choosing your exterior paving, don't for a second be tempted to use an interior tile – exterior tiles are thicker and require a much higher slip rating than what would be specified indoors. Be sure you are choosing paving with a slip rating of R11 or higher, and more like R12 or higher around swimming pools, if possible.

## Think of the future

You have an array of paving materials to choose from, and it's not just about what they look like and what they cost. You need to think about maintenance and longevity. As much as I hate to say it, no material will look perfect forever. Whatever you choose is going to need cleaning and maintaining, so go in with your eyes open and invest in a jet washer.

Also remember to think long term – the shiny, new paving that's just been installed isn't going to stay shiny and new forever. Apart from porcelain, which will remain much the same if it's well cared for and cleaned, paving is going to weather and age, so it's important to consider a material you like the look of when new and when not so new. As a general rule, you can't go far wrong if you choose a stone that is local to your area. Not only does this have a smaller carbon footprint, but it's likely going to work with the house and surroundings. So let me talk you through your options.

# LARGE-FORMAT PAVING

Here I've listed the main materials that can be used for large-format paving. They all have their pros and cons, and I'm not necessarily recommending any one over another, just letting you know what's available. Ultimately, the decision comes down to your preference and what will work best in your particular garden.

## Limestone

### WHAT IS IT?

Limestone is possibly my favourite and I use it in many of my projects. It's a sedimentary rock made of calcium carbonate composed of compacted shells, organisms, and algae over millions of years. I absolutely love the fossils in the stone, which add real character and soul.

### WHY USE IT?

Limestone is slightly less porous than sandstone, so it's less likely to stain – although it will stain if you don't clean it – and the colours tend to be much more consistent. It's available in varying tones from buttery buffs to pale and darker greys. Limestone tends to cost slightly more than sandstone. It can have quite a smooth finish, so do check slip ratings to ensure you are using one suitable for outdoor use.

## Granite

### WHAT IS IT?

Granite is an igneous rock that is incredibly tough and resistant, which is why you so often see it in setts (square cobbles) on driveways and in public schemes. You can tell it's granite by the slightly speckly and sparkly finish to it.

### WHY USE IT?

It is a hard-wearing beast that is great for high-traffic areas, but it can feel quite municipal. Its tough nature and aesthetic often suit more contemporary schemes.

## Porcelain

### WHAT IS IT?

Porcelain paving is essentially a clay tile that is printed with a very high-resolution image to replicate the look of stone, wood, or patterns to very convincing effect. It has low water absorption, which means it can be very slippery if the slip rating isn't high enough – so be sure to choose a grippy option with a high slip rating to avoid accidents, and whatever you do, don't use an interior option.

### WHY USE IT?

Porcelain's best feature, in my view, is how easy it is to clean. One jet wash and it's back to almost new, making it a great choice for more shady areas or contemporary schemes. That said, it also has downsides: being a manufactured and printed product, it can lack a little soul, and it won't age with your garden, which can make it jar with more natural materials and in rural settings. Its use is also more limited – as a printed tile, the colour doesn't go through the entire slab, making your choice for coping stones, steps, and edging more restricted where it needs to be glued together to create a side profile. It also presents a problem if you happen to chip the stone, revealing the white tile beneath.

## Sandstone

### WHAT IS IT?

Sandstone is a sedimentary rock made up of, you guessed it, sand. It's got a good slip resistance, so its grippy texture makes it great for around swimming pools, hot tubs, and ice baths (yes, really) and for more general paving. It's a porous stone and can stain and go green quickly, so it's not something I like to use in north-facing spots, where the shade will encourage algae growth.

### WHY USE IT?

Colours can range from buffs and browns to greys and even orangey reds, which means you can end up with a patchwork effect or strong bands of colour unless you choose one of the more even-toned sawn options (see p78). It is probably the most commonly used paving stone in gardens because it can be a very affordable option, although it can also be a very expensive option if you go for one of my favourites – a beautiful York stone, a type of sandstone quarried in Yorkshire in England. Cheap sandstones are often quarried in India and not always ethically – so please do your homework on where it's sourced from.

## Bluestone/basalt

### WHAT IS IT?

Bluestone, also known as basalt, is a type of dense, fine-grained rock prized for its blue-grey colour and natural cleft surface.

### WHY USE IT?

Bluestone is durable and resistant to staining but may require sealing every two to three years to maintain its appearance over time.

## Concrete

### WHAT IS IT?

Ok, this isn't a stone but it is an option for paving, and can either be cast *in situ* or precast in any given shape.

### WHY USE IT?

Concrete is highly durable, hard wearing, and, other than the polished kind, is very slip resistant. That said, it's also very porous and prone to staining, so it will need treating. Concrete paving can be either very premium or very affordable, depending on what you choose. Contemporary, large-format precast units can command high price tags, but you can also buy inexpensive small-format versions, which, I must admit, are not overly attractive.

## Slate

### WHAT IS IT?

Slate is a metamorphic rock that is durable and stain resistant. It's impervious to water, which is why it's used as a roofing material, but can make for a very slippery (and dangerous) surface.

### WHY USE IT?

It's not a stone I use often. It can be prone to cracking and chipping, so it works better as a decorative aggregate or laid on edge as a feature.

Here 900 x 600mm (36 x 24in) porcelain was used to bring a contemporary feel to the space and complement the flooring used in the rooms that adjoin the garden.

## PAVING SLAB SIZES

You also need to consider the paving size and laying pattern:

| FORMAT | SIZE |
| --- | --- |
| Standard rectangle | 900 x 600mm (36 x 24in) |
| Standard square | 600 x 600mm (24 x 24in) |
| Project pack | mix of 900 x 600mm (36 x 24in), 600 x 600mm (24 x 24in), 600 x 290mm (24 x 12in), and 290 x 290mm (12 x 12in) slabs |

Note that exterior tiles are thicker than interior ones. Typical exterior natural stone paving is supplied at 30mm (1¼in) thick and exterior porcelain at 20mm (¾in). Don't be tempted to use thinner, internal options, as they won't withstand the weather and external conditions, and the slip rating won't be sufficient.

I like the aesthetic of the rectangular format over the square, which can feel a little too symmetrical to me, but there are times when squares work well, depending on what's going on indoors. Project packs are more common with sandstones, and this creates more of a patchwork effect as a result of the varying sizes.

If you have a long, narrow garden, choose rectangular pavers and lay them with the wider edge running across the garden, which will give a feeling of width. Running the wider edge up the garden makes it feel even longer and narrower.

# SMALL-FORMAT PAVING

I love to mix up paving by adding in a smaller-format element, whether it be to divide a space, edge a path, or create a more intimate and delineated space within a larger paved area. This is where small-format pavers come into their own. Clay pavers, cobbles and setts for pathways, driveway edges, decorative "rugs" or rumble strips in a drive, stepping stones, and so much more add texture and interest that can't be achieved in the same way by the larger-format pavers.

You can have fun with the colours of these too. Choosing a matching colour in a smaller format usually creates a very elegant and discreet contrast. Or you can mix up the colours, choosing something lighter or darker if you want a more impactful contrast. The beauty of these smaller formats is they can often be laid with kiln-dried sand between them, allowing for excellent drainage and permeability (and the possibility of some self-seeded surprises that you may or may not want). You have several options to choose from.

## Clay pavers

### WHAT ARE THEY?

Oh, how I love a clay paver, as does much of the design industry. These clay bricks are fired at high temperatures in a kiln for strength. They are available in a variety of lengths and often originate from the Netherlands, where clay pavers are very popular as a build material.

### WHY USE THEM?

Clay pavers are a brilliant option for adding some interest in the garden in an elegant and classic way. They come in an enormous variety of colours, from yellows and greys to blacks, reds, and browns. A lovely material to use, they are usually installed with kiln-dried sand between, creating an attractive, permeable surface that ages into a charming and characterful appearance. I love to use these in pathways instead of larger-format units in both modern and traditional schemes.

## Cobblestones

### WHAT ARE THEY?

Usually made from limestone or sandstone, cobblestones can be square, rectangular, or rounded.

### WHY USE THEM?

Goodness me, I love a rustic cobble. I use them in driveways where I want to evoke that stableyard feel, as rumble strips to break up great swathes of gravel in drives, as edging, or as thresholds beneath driveway gates, and in pathways to create a rustic feel. They aren't very high-heel friendly, so they are best used where foot traffic is low.

## Setts

### WHAT ARE THEY?

Setts are usually square or rectangular units of stone. They can be made from granite, concrete, sandstone, or limestone.

### WHY USE THEM?

Granite or concrete setts (that is, block pavers) are most commonly used in high-traffic areas such as driveways and pathways due to their hard-wearing nature. Although they aren't the prettiest choice, they do the job and are particularly useful in sloping sites, where gravel wouldn't work as it would just fall down the slope.

## Pitchers, tuckers, stackers, or batts

### WHAT ARE THEY?

Stone merchants use different words, but these are all names for a similar style of small-format paving that is usually made of limestone or sandstone. They can often be made out of the same or similar stone as your larger-format paving. Essentially, they are small versions of large-format paving, in the shape of a narrow brick.

### WHY USE THEM?

They are a lovely way to mix up the textures in a garden without going too contrasty, and they can also work brilliantly as risers for steps.

## Crazy paving

### WHAT IS IT?

Crazy paving is a type of irregular paving, usually made from sandstone or limestone.

### WHY USE IT?

I keep hearing crazy paving is making a comeback, but at the time of writing, the 1970s style of crazy paving is still not for me. That said, there are some very chic irregular paving options, often seen at RHS Chelsea, which are fabulous. They have the spirit of crazy paving without the DIY, chunky grout gaps of their predecessors. Irregular paving can also work laid in gravel as stepping stones, or as irregular shapes with an abundance of plants tumbling forth – this is a lovely way to use offcuts and leftovers (sustainability and waste limitation are the name of the game).

## Creasing tiles

### WHAT ARE THEY?

A creasing tile is typically a clay tile used for roofing, usually red but very occasionally yellow/buff. Creasing tiles are having a moment. They aren't new, far from it – go to Great Dixter and you have a feast of creasing tiles to swoon over – but they are definitely featuring more often in designed gardens of late.

### WHY USE THEM?

You can use them as a decorative element in a garden, whether laid on top of each other as a riser in a step, or laid on edge as a decorative feature – these are particularly charming in gardens of Arts and Crafts properties, where creasing tiles are often seen on the house.

# PAVING PATTERNS

There are many different paving patterns to choose from, depending on your preference, style of garden, and paving material. Here is a selection of some of the most commonly used patterns for large- and small-format paving.

## LARGE-FORMAT PAVING

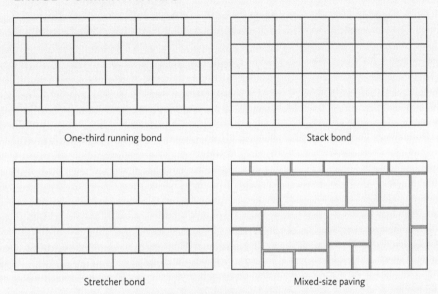

One-third running bond

Stack bond

Stretcher bond

Mixed-size paving

## SMALL-FORMAT PAVING

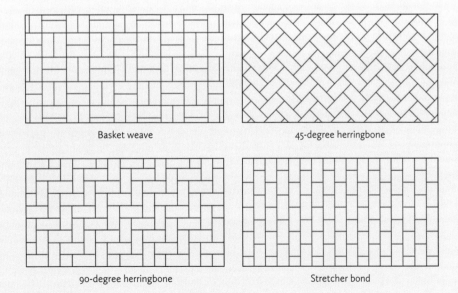

Basket weave

45-degree herringbone

90-degree herringbone

Stretcher bond

## Sealing and drainage

Sealing natural stone divides opinion: some say it makes maintenance of the paving easier and helps to prevent stains impregnating the stone too deeply; others think it better just to let the stone age. That said, sealing won't prevent staining completely – it just makes cleaning easier than with an unsealed stone.

Don't forget to factor in drainage when installing any hard landscaping elements. When laying paving, for example, you need to make sure that it has a "fall" to it. This means a gentle gradient that directs the surface water to run off in a designated direction, whether that be into a border, lawn, or drain. Do check with the stone supplier what the recommended fall of your chosen paving is, as it varies from material to material. Likewise, if you want a level threshold between the paving and the house, you will need to ensure you have drainage. This can be a slimline slot drain or something chunkier, and it's best you take advice on this from the landscaper.

## A seamless transition

Having a seamless, level transition from interior to exterior is a popular concept and a building requirement in new builds. To achieve this, you need to ensure that your damp course is a minimum of 150mm (6in) above your planned exterior ground level. You will also need a drainage channel between the door threshold and paving. It's important to ensure your paving has a fall ratio of between 1:40 and 1:60 away from the house to ensure all water falls away from the doorway. If in doubt, do get a landscaper in to assist – this isn't something to cut corners on.

## Sawn or riven?

Not only do you need to choose your paving, you also need to choose your finish. "Sawn" means exactly that – the stone has been sawn to a smooth finish. Riven stone has a more undulating surface. There are lots of other finishes to look out for, from honed and washed to etched, which vary the texture and colour of the stone. Have a good browse and be sure to order samples.

Sawn paving (far left) lends a contemporary feel to a scheme, while riven surfaces (left) are lovely in more traditional settings.

DEVELOPING YOUR DESIGN

## Don't forget grout

A bad grout job – or pointing, as it's otherwise known – can ruin my day, as well as the look of a garden. I absolutely despise a chunky grout gap or a heavy contrast. Bleurgh. So, to help you avoid my ire, here's a handy guide to grouting.

As a general rule, I like to choose a grout that is the same tone as the paving. We are not looking to create a dark or bright contrasting border around each paver, but turn it into something that looks consistent to the eye across the terrace. To that end, don't just let whoever is installing the paving make this choice for you. Be a diva and choose your own grout colour. This is a long-term decision and not the time for indifference.

You also need to get the grout gap size right. This is usually listed on the supplier website, so do check, but here are some guidelines:

| PAVING | GROUT GAP |
|---|---|
| Traditional-style paving where the edge profile is riven | 8–10mm (⅜–½in) |
| More contemporary paving with a sleeker sawn profile | 3–5mm (⅛–¼in) |

# DECKING

There is decking, and then there is decking. I'm sure we have all seen our fair share of rotten old decking, more slippery than an ice rink and bowing underfoot. But decking can be brilliant with the right materials and care. I love to use it in woodland schemes as a walkway, or as a floating platform over tricky slopes, or as a yoga platform by outbuildings. It's also incredibly useful for roof terraces and balconies, or where we have to build up rather than down. Do watch out though – if you are planning on introducing a raised deck, you must check your local planning rules if you want to build up.

There is a choice of a smooth or grooved/reeded finish. Smooth looks better, in my view, and I am not an enormous fan of the ubiquitous grooved option, as it gathers dirt and leaves and I just don't like the finish as much. However, it's arguably less slippery and handy for around hot tubs (when kept clean). For materials, you can opt for softwood, hardwood, or composite.

## Softwood decking

Softwood is the cheapest option but also the quickest to rot, and it's usually but not always made of pine. It has a relatively short lifespan, and will need annual treating and preserving to maintain it, but there are some options that have been heat treated to improve the lifespan.

## Hardwood decking

Hardwood decks are hard wearing and long lasting – your options include ipe, iroko, oak, chestnut, and many others. It's important you make sure that whichever one you choose is harvested responsibly and certified by the Forest Stewardship Council (FSC). This ensures that the wood comes from ethically sourced, well-managed forests that prioritize sustainability. If you want the deck to remain similar in tone to when it was laid, you will need to oil it annually, so it's not without maintenance.

## Composite decking

Composite decking can be a great option if you are worried about maintenance or discoloration. As with real timber decking, you get what you pay for, and I am not a fan of the cheap plastic ones, for obvious reasons. The good composite decks are usually made from a combination of wood fibres and resin or similar binding agents, and come in a wide variety of colours. My preferred options are those that emulate the look of natural wood, with a smooth surface rather than the grooved finish, which can look a bit artificial.

The beauty of a composite deck is it needs far less maintenance, from cleaning to oiling, and it's much less likely to rot. You have the option of choosing pale grey or buff varieties that pair beautifully with natural stone, as well as the typical dark brown, which can bring a lovely warmth. The darker decks can get rather hot underfoot in the summer, so steer clear of the very dark options in the sunniest spots.

You have a number of options for material and tone when choosing your decking.

# STEPS AND RAMPS

When it comes to steps, you have myriad choices as to what you use for the tread. If you want a clean and consistent aesthetic, then you can't go wrong using the same large-format paving on your steps as on your terraces, whether that be natural stone, concrete, or porcelain.

## Step treads and edges

One thing to consider when looking at your steps is the finish of the step edge. You have a variety of options. In natural stone, you can choose from bullnose and half bullnose to pencil round, chamfer, and downstand. For porcelain, many of the same options apply, but given the colour of a porcelain tile doesn't follow through the entirety of the slab, there will be a visible seam and/or a colour change in the bullnose option, so a downstand is often the preferred alternative to avoid this. You can also add a shadow gap, which is where steps appear to float above one another and is even more impactful when lit.

You can also add some interest to the steps by mixing up the materials and using a smaller format such as clay pavers, brick, or creasing tiles (see pp74–76) – these work best where they feature in the garden or house already, so they repeat in multiple spaces.

## Step risers

The risers are usually made of stone, blocks, brick, or concrete, but that doesn't mean they need to be the visible face material. Risers can be faced with creasing tiles, natural stone, or porcelain, or metal or clay pavers/stackers. This can be a lovely detail to tie in to the rest of the garden if you feature a smaller-format paver elsewhere and then use it as a step riser too.

## Ramps

You can also consider including ramps in your garden instead of or in addition to steps. They will ensure accessibility for all and are a useful route for wheelchairs and wheelbarrows. Note that ramps will need seven times more horizontal space than steps.

Steps can be made from a variety of materials, and you can either match the riser to the step tread, as shown opposite, top and bottom left, or you can use an alternative material, such as opposite, top and bottom right.

# WALLS

There is nothing I love more than a walled garden. For me, it is the gardening holy grail and would be number one on my dream garden wishlist. But for those of us not so lucky to have a *bona fide* walled garden, there may still be areas of your garden that require a wall – whether for a boundary, as a retaining wall, or dividing a space. Regardless of its use, you have options as to the materials.

## Brick walls

Whether the bricks are new or reclaimed, this is a classic choice. My advice is always to make sure your walls work in harmony with the house, so keep those colours as similar as possible, and if you can use the same brick, all the better. Reclaimed bricks are gorgeous at instantly adding character, but they come at a premium, both in terms of cost and labour to lay them. When it comes to laying patterns, there are a number of brick bonds you can choose from, from running bond to common, English, and, my favourite, Flemish bond.

## Blockwork walls

Concrete blocks are often the most economical solution because they are cheap to buy and quick to install, but these aren't just left as is – they need to be clad in stone/timber or porcelain, or rendered to create an acceptable finish (bare concrete blocks are not a look). Where budgets are tight and walls are essential, a blockwork wall that is rendered, or that you paint and plant evergreen hedging in front of, is the most economical solution. Do watch out with render – in paler tones, it often shows up green drip marks that will need cleaning, and it can also blow, meaning the render chips and falls off, which looks less than ideal. Darker colours of render tend to be more forgiving, and in the UK, I avoid white at all costs – it just turns to shades of green so quickly with wet weather – but in hotter climates (think Santorini!), it is utterly fabulous.

## Stone walling and cladding

I love to use local stone to clad walls in a garden – it always feels like it belongs when it's sourced locally. Stone walls can be made a number of ways, from a traditional dry-stone wall to knapped flint and cladding the face of a blockwork wall.

## Sleeper walls

These walls are made from large timber beams called sleepers. These are a really cost-effective way of creating a retaining wall, although they do have a limited lifespan and will eventually rot. They work best in more informal designs, as they can look odd in more minimalist or modern schemes, where their very natural aesthetic fights with cleaner, more contemporary elements.

## Gabion walls

Gabion walls are composed of rocks, cobbles, bricks, or even tiles that are piled into metal gabions – essentially cubes of wire. These are a relatively cost-efficient way of creating a retaining wall, and they work best in more relaxed designs.

The type of wall you choose will depend on your budget and the aesthetic of the garden. You can always conceal less attractive walls with evergreen planting, or make a feature of other, more striking ones.

The house is constructed with stone in buff and brown tones, so materials for the garden were selected to complement this. The large-format paving picks up the cornerstones of the house, while the clay pavers and gravel are a nod to the walling.

Small-format clay pavers in a complementary buff tone divide up the space, rather than having a sea of paving. The smaller format softens the feel of the terrace.

DEVELOPING YOUR DESIGN

The step treads, risers, and retaining walls are all faced or made with the same limestone as the terrace to create an elegant and understated finish.

A warm-toned gravel with steel edging is used for pathways. This instantly adds a softness and warmth to the hardscaping and provides a more gentle transition to the lawn.

HARDSCAPING

# FENCES AND SCREENS

Fencing is a great solution where you need an instant and solid boundary, and don't have the space, budget, or inclination for brick walls, or, indeed, where you need something more instant (or perhaps more secure) than a hedge. When it comes to the format of the fence, there are two main options – closed or open board, with different styles for each (see below). Where privacy and clear delineation of boundaries are needed, then a closed board fence is the way to go.

Fences are available in a range of styles. You can either buy ready-made panels or have something custom built by your landscaper. Styles include shiplap, feather edge, hit and miss, slats, and tongue and groove. Personally, my favourite in more urban spaces is a tongue and groove fence, largely as it is the easiest to paint and it forms a solid boundary with no gaps or holes. It reminds me of interior panelling, which I am an enormous fan of, and it lends an elegance to a garden that is synonymous with our designs.

## Timber fencing

I much prefer to paint timber fencing as I find the bare, pale timber of a typical fence can be a real eye draw, and in my view, fences are there to act as a boundary, not a focal point. I prefer to paint them a very dark blue, dark green, or black in more urban spaces and then cover them in climbers, so they disappear into the background. It's rare that I want to make a feature of a typical timber fence!

Painting is also a great solution if you have a series of mismatched fence panels (either in style or colour) in the garden – just make sure you own the fence or have permission before painting it (see p41). You aren't limited to the off-the-shelf paints available in DIY stores, either – you can get an outdoor paint mixed up to any colour you like.

The boundary treatment you choose will depend on its purpose. Is it to screen, delineate a boundary, or for plants to climb up?

## Woven willow

Woven willow is a stunning option in both rural and urban spaces, either to top a wall or as an entire fence. It instantly adds a naturalistic element to the garden and can work brilliantly to divide spaces too. However, it's worth noting that it requires reworking around every 10 years or so, and you will need to treat it to maximize its lifespan. You can also look at living willow screens, which are lovely for encircling play spaces.

## Railings

When it comes to more rural, country gardens, hedging nearly always looks better than a solid fence. We will often install a near-imperceptible metal fence alongside a hedge if we need to keep dogs in (or deer out), for example. There are also more open fence options, such as a post-and-rail fence; estate fencing, which works well where privacy is not needed but delineation of a boundary is; or picket fencing, which is frankly just adorable.

# EDGING

I always like a crisp, neat edge for lawns, paths, and planting borders, as not only does it look lovely, it also cuts down on maintenance, preventing the spread of grass and weeds and saving you the backbreaking work of cutting in lawn edges year on year. You can introduce edging to the garden in a number of ways, and what you choose will depend on your budget and the look and feel of your garden.

## Lawn and planting borders

My preferred go-to for lawn and borders is a steel edge, which you can install at a 3mm (⅛in) or 6mm (¼in) thickness: 3mm (⅛in) is better for curves as it allows more bend, and 6mm (¼in) is better for straight lines. You can have this in a mild steel, which will age down to a dark brown in six to 12 months, or you can go for a Corten steel, rust look, or powder coated if you have a specific colour in mind. Timber edging is an alternative solution, but bear in mind this will rot in time, so it's not something I tend to use. You can also edge lawns with brick, small-format pavers, or stone, which can look absolutely lovely in the right scheme – it really does depend on what look you are trying to achieve.

## Gravel pathways

You have lots of choice for gravel pathways, from a metal or timber edge, as above, or alternatively, a brick, stacker, cobble, or sett. What you choose will depend on what you are using elsewhere in the garden. Metal gives a minimalist and sleek finish, whereas cobbles, clay pavers, and stackers can add a touch of formality and elegance to a path and have a more traditional feel.

## What to choose?

There are a few factors to consider when choosing your edging.

**Style** It's important to choose a material that matches the overall style of the garden. For a traditional look, go with brick, clay paving, or stone edging for paths, or you can opt for steel if you want it to disappear beneath planting tumbling over it. For something more modern, steel is perfect, or a slim, formal paver. In more naturalized settings such as a woodland, timber can be lovely, albeit it won't last as long.

**Functionality and shape** If your borders are curved, a flexible steel is going to be far easier to install, whereas bricks and pavers are fine with straight lines.

**Budget** The labour to install natural stone is going to make it one of the most costly options, and while steel is not cheap, it's quicker to install, so your budget may influence your decision.

Edging can take many forms, from timber and metal to stone.

Sculpture at the centre of the garden acts as a focal point and gives the gravel strip purpose.

Despite the garden being quite shallow, generous borders give the illusion of depth and blur the boundaries, so it's not so obvious where the garden ends.

DEVELOPING YOUR DESIGN

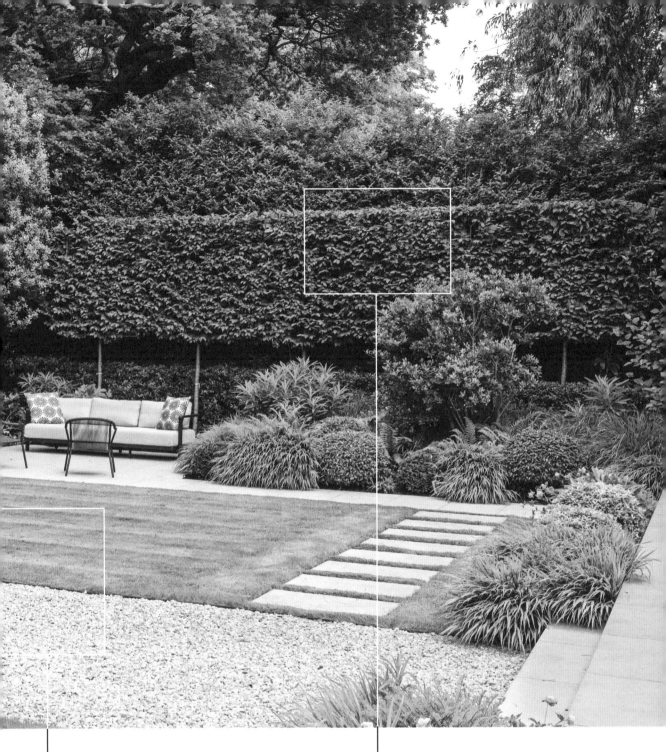

The lawn, which is much wider than it is deep, is bisected with a generous gravel strip to give a feeling of depth to the garden. Cutting across a space is a great way to make it feel wider.

Pleached hornbeam (*Carpinus*) trees add an extra layer of privacy on the boundary and a feeling of immersion in the corner of the garden.

# WHAT TO USE WHERE

So now you've picked your materials, how do you decide what to use where? When you're looking at materials, remember to consider the use of each space in terms of footfall, maintenance, furniture, and light. Shade can really impact the weathering of natural materials, encouraging algae growth that can lead to greening, so bear it in mind as we work through the options. Let's look at various areas you might be considering.

## Dining and seating spaces

Where possible, aim for anywhere that houses furniture to have a hard surface such as large-format paving, small-format pavers, or decking. Anything with an uneven surface, such as gravel or very textural cobbles, can make furniture wobble. That said, there are always exceptions to the rule, and a grand dining space on a compressed gravel base à la south of France can be dreamy in the right setting – but most find the gravel movement under chairs a little annoying.

You can also mix up your materials in dining and seating spaces with large-format paving and a small-format "rug" within, for example, or a smaller-format border or pattern. Now take note here – this works brilliantly when you are certain of your furniture position and you have methodically measured it all out, but it can be disastrous if the feature doesn't accommodate all the furniture. So be sure to do your homework with furniture sizes and, if in doubt, go bigger with the paving – just not too big.

## Pathways

Pathways can be made up of large-format paving, small-format pavers or bricks, gravel, resin-bound gravel, or even bark. What you use will depend on who or what will be using the pathway. Will it just be you, or might there be wheelchairs, wheelbarrows, bikes, buggies, or luggage on wheels? If the latter, you might want to consider the more solid options, which allow for an easier ride. You can also mix and match your materials here, such as mixing large- and small-format versions of the same paving to break up the length of the path, or using cobbles or bricks as an edging to a gravel path.

Large-format limestone in a stretcher bond was used for this dining space to allow for a comfortable and even surface for furniture.

## Driveways

Your choice of materials for driveways are block pavers, bricks, cobbles, gravel, tarmac, or resin-bound gravel. There are pros and cons to each of these, from costs to drainage. Gravel is my preferred material – it just has a softness that other materials don't provide, and it helps that it's the most drainage and cost friendly, as well as its crunchy sound being a handy security feature. Some don't like the migration of the pebbles, but this can be counteracted with stabilization grids and by choosing a chunkier stone (see p68) – we aren't trying to re-create Brighton beach. If your garden is on a slope, gravel can be tricky, so this is where the alternatives such as block paving, cobbles, setts, or tarmac come into play.

## Swimming pools and hot tubs

The most important thing to consider around pools and hot tubs is the slip rating. This is not the place for a super-smooth porcelain – around pools, you need a nice grippy stone, porcelain, or decking with a high slip rating. If you want to use a natural stone, sandstone is a great choice as it's grippy underfoot thanks to the sandy texture, and limestone can work well just as long as it's got a good slip rating.

Porcelains can vary in slip rating, so if you're planning to put it around a pool, make sure you choose one with the highest slip rating possible. With decking, you can choose a natural timber or a composite – both are naturally grippy underfoot, just as long as you keep them clean and leaf free.

# SUSTAINABILITY

I couldn't write a chapter on materials without talking about
sustainability. In our changing climate, it is imperative that sustainable
and environmentally sensitive choices are at the heart of all design, and
that we are mindful of the carbon footprint of the materials we choose.
There are a number of factors you can consider to create a more
sustainable garden. I have only touched on a topic with myriad possibilities,
and there are brilliant resources to read if you want to learn more.

## Reused and reclaimed materials

You do not need to start from scratch. If your paving is in a good condition, and
could be reused after a clean or by lifting and relaying, then please do consider
doing that. If, for whatever reason, you can't or don't want to reuse it, don't throw
it in a skip – ask your contractor whether paving can be reused as part of the build
as an aggregate or foundation. Or perhaps it could be donated to a reclamation
yard – remember, we are trying to avoid materials going to landfill.

You don't need to use brand-new materials in the garden if you can't reuse
what you already have. Reclamation yards are a treasure trove of paving, bricks,
and tiles that can be added to the garden to give them a second life. Reclaimed
doesn't mean horrible, either – just look at one of the most expensive materials out
there, reclaimed York stone, to see that old and used doesn't mean undesirable.

## Permeability

Remember to consider permeability when choosing materials. Using gravel
rather than solid paving allows water to pass through and be absorbed into
the ground instead of creating excessive runoff. Small unit pavers pointed
with sand rather than mortar have a similar effect, as does introducing planting
channels within paved areas.

## Go local

The more you can source your materials locally, the fewer kilometres they've
had to travel, reducing their carbon footprint. Buying locally also supports local
businesses, which is a bonus.

# Harvest rainwater

This is such a simple win for us all, and it can be as simple or as high tech as you wish. Start by installing water butts to your downpipes to store water runoff from roofs to use in the summer months. If you have the resources, installing attenuation tanks, which gather rainwater either above or below ground, is a brilliant way of storing water on a larger scale to use in irrigation systems. You can also consider using recycled, or grey, water, such as from the bath, shower, or kitchen, to irrigate your plants in the short term, but don't use grey water on fruit and vegetable crops because it may contain pathogens.

# No to plastic

Try not to use plastic in any form, and that includes artificial turf. It's terrible for the environment, soil, and wildlife. Many nurseries now supply plants in recyclable pots, which are grey or beige rather than black, or coir containers. If you do buy plants with non-recyclable pots, reuse them or donate them to a garden. Don't put them in a skip.

# SUDS

Sustainable drainage systems (SUDS) manage surface water runoff by mimicking natural drainage processes. There are various techniques for this, including using permeable surfaces that allow water to infiltrate the ground, such as gravel or permeable paving; using green roofs to absorb rainwater and reduce runoff; and introducing swales, which are shallow channels or ditches that capture runoff.

# Add more plants

There is nothing that makes my heart sink more than a request for a garden with minimal plants. Apart from the design perspective, it's a wasted opportunity to invite wildlife into the garden. Whether it's food for pollinators or shelter for insects, planting is adding to the planet in a way that paving takes away. Try to choose plants that don't require heavy irrigation (although they will likely need some in year one to establish) – so resilient plants that can withstand wet winters and dry summers. See more on this in the planting section on pp134–35 and 147.

# TIPS ON CHOOSING MATERIALS

So I have given you all your options, but what should you choose? The answer is – it depends on everything we've looked at previously regarding your wishlist and your specific garden in terms of locale, architecture, and use. Remember to reuse materials or use reclaimed materials where you can (see p96).

## Traditional-style garden

If you want a traditional-style garden, then go for traditional materials. Think natural, riven stone – potentially in varied size formats rather than crisp, uniform sizes – and cobbles, bricks, or creasing tiles for smaller elements.

## Modern country garden

If you want a modern country garden, then you can go a little more contemporary with the materials, and we can bring in the "country" with the planting. Go for buff tones and avoid the greys, and don't be scared to mix it up with smaller-format versions of the same material or those with a similar colour tone.

## Ultramodern garden

If you want to go ultramodern and minimalist, consider grey paving or concrete in large formats with minimal small-format elements. Head back to your moodboard (see pp24–25) and match your materials to the aesthetic you wanted at the start.

## Inspiration from the house

If you're still stuck on what to choose, a really good place to start is to take inspiration from the house. What colour is it? What's it made from? What colour is the pointing in the bricks? Does it have timber elements, cladding, or maybe tiles? Now, this doesn't mean if you have a red-brick house I am suggesting you have red paving – that would be *a lot*. But notice the brick pointing colour – is it a buff yellow? In which case, maybe look at buff-toned paving that will complement that and help tie the two together. We have also been known to match window frames, roof tiles, pretty elements such as creasing tiles, even timber panelling – the trick is to pick complementary materials.

Here, small-format sawn cobbles were chosen for this transitional space. A sawn option was selected as it's a high-foot-traffic area, and the cobbles are a nod to the previous use of the site as a kennels and stableyard.

## Location, location, location

Remember where you are. We talked about *genius loci* and location before (see p20). Don't fight it. If you live in a rural location with an old house, a pale grey porcelain is going to look weird. Likewise, oldy-worldy cobbles are going to look a bit nuts with an ultramodern house. Work with what you have, and if you can, source your materials from local quarries and mills. If it's a local stone, chances are it's going to work.

## Less is more

We try to limit material choices to no more than three. We might pick one large-format paving, one small-format paving, and a gravel. You do not need more than one of each – you can always use the same material in different sizes and patterns to keep things interesting.

## Repeat, repeat, repeat

One of the most elegant ways of tying the design of a garden together is to use the same material in different ways throughout a garden. We might use a stacker (see p75) as a step riser and repeat it as the main material in a pathway, as a feature "rug" within paving, or as the base beneath a feature bench. The trick is to repeat the materials around the garden, so there is a continuous thread at varying points.

## Be practical

Think about your specific garden and how much you are going to dedicate (or pay someone else) to keeping it looking good. Are you really going to jet wash it every weekend or would it be wiser to choose a more forgiving option that hides the dirt, dog footprints, and so on?

## Order samples

Most stone suppliers will happily send you samples, which you can take outside to the spot you plan to use them. Put them on the ground where they will actually be – don't go judging them from a table! Get them wet too, as some stones can

The cobbles seen here repeat around the garden in various transitional spaces. The steps and coping stones of the walls also repeat, tying all the elements together.

DEVELOPING YOUR DESIGN

change colour dramatically when wet, and if you live in rainier parts of the world, you'd better like it both wet and dry. If you're really committed, stand on it too. Does it feel nice underfoot? I have been known to take my shoes off at showrooms to get a feel for it. Go on, I dare you.

## Visit showrooms

Visit showrooms to see paving laid *in situ*. This is really worth doing, as a small sample can look very different from a large laid area. With natural stone, it will also allow you to see the variations in colour, of which there are often many.

## Avoid very pale stone

Bright, white paving might seem like a lovely idea, but it's going to be blindingly bright in the summer sun and a nightmare to clean in the winter. My advice is, don't do it.

# Materials moodboard

Once you have chosen all your materials, lay them all out to make sure they work together, either as images on your computer, or better, as real stone/material samples. Put them next to your house on the ground and step back – do they work nicely together? Is it all working as a combination, or is something jarring as not quite right?

# Fitting it all in

I have an optional exercise for you here, but it's really worth doing if you have an eye for detail and want a really accurate and slick design. Now that you have chosen your materials, you should know the dimensions of each, and so we can adapt your garden design so they fit without any awkward leftover bits. This is why it's so important to draw the garden up to scale.

So, for example, if you have chosen your paving and it comes in a 900 x 600mm (36 x 24in) rectangle, you can now map this on your plan. You can change the dimensions of the paved space so your materials fit into the design in a way that means minimal cuts to the paving and, more importantly, no awkward little slivers of stone left over. This doesn't have to be to the millimetre, but try to work with a multiple of the paving dimensions – it's going to look so much better than if you don't bother.

Most good landscapers will do this for you without you even knowing – it's just good practice. So take the time to redraw your plan, reflecting the dimensions of the hard materials you're using. It's one of the fun things about designing a garden instead of an interior – we can tweak the layout of the space based on the materials we use. Don't worry if you end up with a few cuts – the real thing we are looking to avoid is tiny leftover bits that just look badly thought out.

5

# THE FINISHES

STORAGE, WATER FEATURES, PERGOLAS AND ARBOURS,
OUTDOOR KITCHENS, FIRE FEATURES, SWIMMING POOLS,
PLAY SPACES, FURNITURE, AND LIGHTING

So you have your concept plan and your materials. Now we can
flesh out the details of everything else that will go into the garden,
from pergolas and ponds to play spaces, and everything in between.

# STORAGE

It's fair to say that most gardens require some level of storage, and the size of it will be dictated by your plot. In smaller spaces, I beg clients to relinquish the need for a huge shed that will gather paint pots and detritus, and streamline to the bare minimum. Of course, garden tools need to be stored somewhere, but if space is tight, then I always advise handing over as little as possible to a shed – so be brutal. Do you need those old kids' toys and 400 plant pots? Can you store bikes in a bike shed in the front garden or in a garage? Push yourself and be strict – sheds are an eyesore, and I've never walked into a garden and admired the copious amounts of storage.

## What about the cushions?

This is one of the most common questions I get asked in regards to storage, and there is no magic bullet on this one. My advice to clients these days is buy furniture with weatherproof cushions that can withstand some summer rain, and some robust furniture covers that you keep nearby. Rather than spend your life monitoring the weather forecast and screeching into the garden at the first sign of rain to shove multiple cushions in a shed, just whack on the covers when not in use and forget about it. When winter comes, cushions need storing, and if possible, they are far better somewhere like a garage, loft, or spare cupboard (who has a spare cupboard?). At worst, they can be stacked in a shed over winter, but they often succumb to spiders, mice, and damp if not protected.

## Out of sight

I've said it once and I'll say it again: if you can avoid putting the shed in the line of sight from the house, please do so. You could paint it black so it recedes into the background (unless you go for a very ornamental posh shed, which is a feature in its own right), and then plant in front of it or install a nice trellis with planting so we can screen the damn thing.

Opt for weatherproof cushions that can withstand the odd summer shower, and keep furniture covers to hand.

# WATER FEATURES

Water is a fabulous addition to the garden, adding white noise that muffles traffic and/or neighbour noise and creating a sense of peace and tranquillity that is hard to beat. The type of water feature you choose will depend on the style and size of your garden. In smaller spaces, I prefer to use more formal features, such as a wall fountain, reflection pool, or bubbling pot, whereas in larger gardens, we can go a bit more free form.

Water features that require pumps can be temperamental and require maintenance, so do consider if you have the appetite for the upkeep. Try to site a water feature away from overhanging trees to prevent leaves falling in the water. If you hope to plant it up, ensure it's positioned where the plants will receive adequate sunlight.

## Reflection pools

These are fabulous in more contemporary schemes, where the reflections of trees and clouds can be seen in the water. They lend such a calming feel to a space and look incredibly chic in minimalist schemes, where the water becomes a sculpture in its own right. You can dye the water with an environmentally and animal-friendly dye, such as Hydra black liquid dye, which amplifies the reflection and suppresses algae growth.

## Rills

My goodness, I love a rill. They lead the eye, divide a space, and are such a special feature in a garden. They need a pump to circulate the water, and can vary in width from a sliver to something far wider. These add a real wow factor to a garden and work particularly well when on multiple levels, with water cascading down each one.

A rill divides areas in this garden and leads the eye to the landscape beyond the boundaries.

A bubbling water feature adds
visual interest to the garden
and can help to mask noise
from traffic or neighbours.

THE FINISHES

# Water bowls

Water bowls are simple, effective, and wildlife friendly and can fit in a garden of any size. They bring a lovely tranquillity to the space and don't need lights or a pump. You will have to replace the water from time to time so it doesn't stagnate.

# Fountains

Fountains can be as large or as small as space allows. A large, circular, tiered fountain in a driveway can look spectacular in the right property – just as long as the scale is right and there is ample room to manoeuvre around it. For smaller spaces, I absolutely love a rustic, wall-mounted fountain. Think National Trust properties and water spurting from the mouth of a lion's head into an old stone trough. Bliss.

The trick with wall fountains is to consider the sound, which will be influenced by the spout – whether it's a tube, blade, or multiple spouts – and the water pressure from the pump. A loud, gushing fountain is brilliant at drowning out noise, but it's also brilliant at sending you to the WC, so consider the placement and water flow carefully.

# Bubbling features

A bubbling water feature adds wonderful white noise to a space. It can be made from any number of vessels, depending on the look of your garden, from gorgeous reclaimed stone basins and troughs to terracotta pots and stone water bowls, to the crisper, clean lines of a steel trough. This style of water feature usually requires a reservoir to allow the water to recirculate, which is usually situated beneath the feature and will need energy to power the pump.

# Ponds

Ponds are fantastic for attracting wildlife, and the art of a good pond is to make it feel like it's always been there. As with any open body of water, they come with a danger to children (see below). In smaller ponds, you can add a grate below the surface, or you can fence it off – this can be a bit of an eyesore, so consider carefully if this is the right feature for you. Be sure to include either a beach or small ramps to allow wildlife to climb in and out.

## A NOTE ON SAFETY

Open bodies of water such as ponds and lakes are wonderful for wildlife but, of course, come with a risk of drowning for small children. So if you want to include one in your garden, be sure to plan how you will mitigate the risk with fencing, gates, or grids. The thought of my children hosting a playdate near an open body of water is enough to freak me out – so do consider who will use your garden (see p12).

# PERGOLAS
# AND ARBOURS

Pergolas and arbours are a wonderful way to add height, shade, and interest to a garden. They can act as a shade cover for specific areas or for walkways and give the opportunity to add in more planting on a vertical plane. Traditionally, they are made of timber, although there are an increasing number of metal versions on the market, with all-singing, all-dancing mechanized louvre roof slats, which turn them into all-weather pavilions with the flick of a switch.

## Timber or metal?

I must admit that, when it comes to pergolas, I much prefer the timber variety to the more utilitarian metal numbers. After all, I am a designer, and therefore aesthetics are just as important to me as function (and they are both important). The gunmetal grey, chunky metal pergolas on the market are incredibly practical, I agree, but they look rather dominant in all but the most contemporary of schemes, and I like my gardens rather more natural. (Sorry.) But beautiful, intricate, and ornate old metal pergolas that belong in the secret garden? That's a different story.

When it comes to designing your pergola or arches, assuming it's timber, you have a number of choices, from the size of the structure, the timber, the thickness of the posts, and the finish of the rafters. The size and shape will be determined by your garden and the furniture it needs to accommodate. I always prefer a chunky timber post – 150mm (6in) and over – to anything too skinny, which can feel a bit half hearted. So don't be scared to give it a little heft.

### Hardwood or softwood?

Much like decking, you have a choice of hard- or softwood, and I would always advise you go for a hardwood for longevity, but do watch out – timber that hasn't been treated can leach tannins, which are a water-soluble extract present in wood. When leached out of the timber onto the surface below, tannins look like you have dropped coffee or brown tar on the surface. It can stain surfaces if not removed promptly, so it's worth being aware and considering the surfaces beneath.

## Fixings

It's also worth considering how you fix your timber to the ground. My preference is to mount the posts on a metal foot so that they sit above ground level, rather than digging and concreting them into the ground, thus reducing the risk of rot. All of these things are worth discussing with the carpenter or landscaper building it for you. Or you can do more research if you are building yourself – bravo. Be sure to use stainless-steel screws or nails, as other options will stain the wood.

A pergola in this small urban garden allows plants to be grown vertically, making good use of the space and creating a sense of seclusion.

## SOFTEN WITH CLIMBERS

Depending on the look you want to achieve, you can add some of your favourite climbers (see pp144–46) to a pergola or archway to soften it, or you can leave it bare for something more contemporary.

# OUTDOOR KITCHENS

It is incredibly rare not to find an outdoor kitchen on the wishlist of most clients these days, and it can range from an all-singing, all-dancing kitchen with sink, fridge, multiple cooking methods, and even a beer tap, to something far more pared back, such as a work surface with a barbecue or pizza oven on top or installed inside.

None of these options is cheap, but the thing I like about an outdoor kitchen, in whatever guise, is it lends a sense of purpose to a space, whereas a free-standing barbecue can feel a bit incidental and transient – it's a psychological thing, I suppose, as so much of garden design is.

## Where to site it

Think very carefully about the position of the kitchen. As with most things in life, convenience is key – you won't thank me (or yourself) for positioning your kitchen at the end of the garden when you forget the salad tongs, or after making your fifth journey to take things back to the house. Where it is going needs to be practical and useful for you.

Usually, pretty near the house allows for quick and easy access, and then there is rarely a need to install a sink or fridge as the indoor kitchen is usually close to hand. Where this doesn't apply so much is where the outdoor kitchen is positioned near an outbuilding, or where it's so well equipped with appliances that there is minimal need to head back to the house for forgotten items. One last point – don't go putting your kitchen right up against any planting that's going to get singed with your cooking exploits and be sure to position it on a hard and level surface.

## What's the set-up?

When considering your kitchen set-up, there are a number of options available, and question number one is how do you want to cook? Gas barbecue? Charcoal? Kamado grill? Pizza oven? Argentinian grill? This choice will inform how large you need the kitchen to be and how much prep space you might want around it. Also consider storage cupboards under the work surface, not only for gas canisters and charcoal, but for all-weather crockery, barbecue implements, and so on.

This timber kitchen is positioned close to the interior kitchen for maximum convenience. Timber complements the oak frames of the house.

## Material options

You can either buy a ready-made outdoor kitchen off the shelf (see suppliers on p186) or you can have one custom made by a good carpenter or landscaper. Material options include concrete, timber, or bricks/blockwork. Then there is the work surface, which bamboozles many. We have used polished concrete, Dekton (which is a form of highly compressed stone), porcelain, and stone. Remember it needs to be durable, weather resistant, and easy to clean. Depending on the position, you may also want to create a backsplash if your barbecue, pizza oven, or other heat-producing apparatus is near planting or timber and you need that extra heatproof buffer – just be sure you use materials that are suitable for outdoors.

In small spaces, it can be temping to minimize the planting, but here, a generous planting border is placed in direct view of the large door, so that plants are the first things seen from the house.

THE FINISHES

Given the compact size of the garden and the proximity to the interior dining space, an outdoor dining table is not needed. Instead, minimalist armchairs are used for a morning coffee and general relaxing, making the space much more flexible and open.

Composite decking in a neutral buff grey matches the interior flooring and tackles the level change of the garden. The garden is north facing, so this easy-to-clean deck is also an ideal alternative to natural stone, which can be slippery and turn green quickly in shady spots.

The black kitchen is a nod to the black glazing of the house, and diagonal timbers complement the glazing. A sink is included for washing dishes and muddy football boots.

# FIRE PITS, FIREPLACES, AND FIRE BOWLS

There is something completely lovely about gathering around a fire of an evening. Whether the fuel you use is wood, gas, or bioethanol is up to you and your location – many cities have smoke control regulations, so do check.

## Where to site it

Where you put your fire feature will depend a little on the style of fireplace you want. More formal vertical fireplaces or fire tables can work brilliantly close to the house, where they create the feel of an outdoor living room. For more rustic finishes such as a fire bowl or traditional fire pit, positioning it further into the garden where it has a more camping vibe works better.

Be sure to position fire features well away from overhanging branches or any planting that can be damaged by the flames, or anything remotely combustible. I absolutely love to surround a rustic fire pit with Adirondack chairs – the low-level wooden seats that you often see on an American porch – which are comfy but naturalistic.

## Fuel choices

There are a few things to consider when choosing what fuel to use, including environmental impact, cost, ambience, and warmth, and all fuels have their benefits and disadvantages.

### Wood

Wood has the benefit of being incredibly versatile – you can position it anywhere with no need for a pipe, and it has a high heat output, which makes for cosy evenings. It's a cost-effective option, and your fire pit or fireplace can be as high or low spec as you wish, from a simple stone circle or fire bowl to a very lovely vertical fireplace.

There are some downsides of a wood fire – it's pretty much inevitable wherever you sit around a wood fire that you will eventually find yourself in the "smoke zone". We've all come home from a night around a campfire to have the smell of it linger in clothes and hair for days. It's also not environmentally friendly, given the air pollution it produces, and it can irritate the neighbours.

A dramatic fireplace creates the perfect focal point and gathering space under this pergola. Positioned far from the house, the fireplace and furniture create an instant outdoor room for cosy evenings around the fire.

## Gas

Gas is a super-speedy and clean way of having a fire in the garden that you can control at the flick of a switch, and there are no smoke issues or ash to clean up. But it comes with an upfront cost outlay for installing a gas pipe (unless you're using a canister), and the fire pit itself will inevitably cost more than a simple log one. From a sustainability point of view, we must also be mindful that we're using a nonrenewable natural resource.

## Bioethanol

Bioethanol fires produce a clean, odourless flame without smoke or ash. They don't need a gas line or electric connection, but they tend to produce less heat compared to wood or gas fires, which means they are better for creating ambience rather than warmth.

# SWIMMING POOLS AND PONDS

If you are lucky enough to have the space and budget for a pool, there are myriad options available to you. Do you want a traditional chlorinated pool or a natural filtration system? Swimming pool or swimming pond? It's worth asking yourself how you'll use the pool or pond, as this will inform everything from size to steps and style.

## What's it for?

If the pool is primarily for exercise, then length and depth are key, and steps need to be kept to the side to allow for the maximum length to be used. You might even want to include a jet to swim against. If it's more for play, then the position of steps is up for grabs. Positioning a shallow ledge within the pool can be a great way to add an extra dimension for kids to play in, or steps that span the entire length or breadth of the pool can act as a lovely perching point.

## Where to site it

When considering position, be sure to place the pool away from overhanging trees, and, where possible, try to position the pool on an east-to-west axis, assuming you want to put your sunloungers on the longer, south-facing side to maximize your sunbathing. You may prefer to sit in the late afternoon and evening sun, in which case, be sure to position your furniture in a west-facing spot. As discussed in the materials section, it's absolutely vital you focus on slip rating when choosing the tiles to go around a pool (see p69).

## Pool covers

There really is only one cover we tend to use now, and that's the integrated cover on tracks. It costs the same as a small car, but it's the only one that's safe for children and pets.

As for selecting a cover colour, we try to choose one as similar to the surrounding paving as possible, such as a beigey grey. Avoid the bright blues or greens, which draw the eye. If the pool is covered, I'd personally prefer it to be unnoticeable rather than something that's shouting at you.

## Interior material and colour

In the interior of the pool, you can have large- or small-format stone or porcelain tiles, glass mosaics, fibreglass, PebbleTec (an aggregate pebble finish), or a vinyl liner. What you choose will depend on your budget and the shape and style of the pool, and a good pool company will talk you through your options.

An interesting rule of thumb with colours is the darker the tile, the more natural the water looks, so in more rural spots, we normally suggest going for a coppery brown or dark teal tile. This might sound insane, but it creates a beautiful deep blue that feels far more appropriate in a rural setting than something pale blue and resembling the Mediterranean Sea. If you want a really crisp and pale turquoise (think Maldives beach), then you can't go wrong using a large-format pale buff porcelain tile. It creates a very modern and minimalist aesthetic.

## Swimming ponds

A wildlife-friendly alternative to your traditional swimming pool, swimming ponds are increasing in popularity. While conventional swimming pools use chemicals to kill microorganisms and bacteria, in a natural pool, the purifying properties of plants and microorganisms keep the water clean.

Ponds can be in a traditional round pond style, or you can have an unplanted, non-chemical pool that resembles more of a traditional swimming pool but with biological filters housed in a nearby hut, which can be a good compromise if you want to have a pool cover.

# GREEN ROOFS, CUTTING GARDENS, AND WILDLIFE

We've talked a lot about the harder features in the garden, but let's not forget the softer ones too. From greening up your roofs to assist in water runoff and soften the general building aesthetic, to adding in productive spaces so you can live out your good-life dreams, let's delve into some of your options.

## Green roofs

Green roofs are a great way to manage water runoff, provide habitats for wildlife, and soften the aesthetic of an otherwise plain flat roof, which you might find on a shed, garage, office, or bike store. They also provide natural insulation, reducing heat gain in the summer and heat loss in the winter. Green roofs can be made from a variety of succulents, grasses, wildflowers, and herbs, all of which sit on a number of underlayers consisting of a waterproof membrane, root barrier, drainage layer, filter, and growing medium.

## Cutting gardens and vegetable beds

There aren't many rules for cutting gardens and vegetable beds other than you absolutely must position them in a sunny spot. Most cut flowers require ample sunlight (at least six hours a day) and most vegetables do too, so be sure to position your growing space somewhere with prime sunlight.

These beds can be as decorative or utilitarian as you wish, and their construction will depend on how visible they are. Usually, raised beds are made with timber posts or sleepers, but you can also make them from metal if preferred, which can be powder coated to a colour of your choosing. Be sure to avoid any old railway sleepers soaked in creosote, which aren't safe for vegetable gardens. I am a sucker for a woven willow surround to raised beds in the right setting, but this material will need to be replaced in time (see p89). As far as size goes, just be sure you can reach the middle of the planter from both sides – you don't want to be treading on the earth.

Raised beds made from timber sleepers are a cost-effective and naturalistic way to add a cutting garden or vegetable-growing space to your garden.

# Wildlife-friendly options

Wildlife is one of the joys of having a garden, and it's our job as custodians of the land to help out our wild friends. They, in return, help us by controlling pests, feeding the soil, pollinating our plants, and generally bringing a huge amount of joy. You can help them by providing food, shelter, and water. This can be as low key as including a small bee hotel or bee brick for solitary bees, bug hotels, and log piles for invertebrates, to hedgehog houses, owl and bat boxes, birdbaths, bird feeders, water bowls and ponds, and, of course, oodles of pollinator-friendly planting.

# ALL ABOUT POTS

I have a strict rule with pots – they must be large. There is rarely a space where I think, gosh, I wish the pots were smaller, but there are endless places where I wish they were larger. Large pots allow for more planting, less watering, and more impact.

## Go large

Let's face it, most of us have a load of pots, and usually most of these are far too small. But here's the problem – they drag your eye to the ground, and the only time that smaller pots look good, in my view, are when there are many of them, planted en masse, and either raised on staging or clustered on a table for the same effect. Small pots spotted around on the floor of a paved area look cluttered and half hearted. So everywhere else, bigger really is better. The downside is big pots are expensive and hard to find (see p186).

## Pot materials

Terracotta pots are beautiful, but it can be heartbreaking when they crack in frost, so buy ones that are guaranteed as frost proof. If you do invest, be sure to protect them in the winter by lifting them off the ground and, if you can, move them to a frost-free place. Blanket them with hessian as a back-up.

Chunky clay pots are a beautiful option and one we use a lot, as you can have them made in almost any colour. Powder-coated steel troughs are brilliant for a sleek finish and are relatively lightweight, making them a great choice for roof terraces and balconies. Old reclaimed stone, such as beautiful old cattle troughs or other reclaimed agricultural items, are utter heaven in a rustic scheme.

## TOP POT TIPS

**Either side of a front door,** consider having tall pots that sit around doorknob height, planted with an evergreen dome. This is going to give a really impressive impact and feel like a proper design decision. Try to avoid low-level pots, which will draw the eye to the ground.

**In smaller spaces such as courtyards,** go bigger not smaller. A brilliant feature can be three pots positioned side by side. Bigger doesn't have to be wide and tall – it could mean three tall and narrow pots, or three chunky but shorter ones.

**If you have a pathway or arches,** positioning one chunky pot at the end, planted with a tree or shrub or mass of planting, can be a fabulous focal point in place of a sculpture.

**If you have a lot of paving,** adding chunky pots planted with trees or shrubs can bring greenery closer to the house and solve the problem of areas where you can't plant in the ground.

**Troughs can make great privacy screens** when planted with grasses or shrubs, and they can be used to soften walls that have paving beneath.

These oversized bowls planted with fleabane (*Erigeron*) and agapanthus create a dramatic focal point.

# PLAY SPACES

Trampolines, climbing frames, sandpits, football goals, monkey bars – you name it, I've included it in gardens up and down the country. Here's what I've learned: kids grow up fast, so try not to design your garden around them, or if you really want to, try to plan for what happens next when they abandon the sandpit.

If your kids are small and you want to see them from inside the house, then go for temporary fixtures that can be relocated when they need less monitoring. As a mother of young boys myself, I can assure you that the time when you don't need to supervise them so closely comes around fast, and you will be glad you didn't design the garden around the play equipment.

## Screen or relocate

As we've seen in Chapter 3, it's a good idea to try to keep the play equipment out of the direct line of sight of the house so that it doesn't become an accidental focal point (see p53). You may want to watch the kids play and get enormous enjoyment out of it, and the visual impact may not bother you, in which case skip ahead, but when it comes to screening or disguising the various accoutrements of kids' play, I have a few tricks I like to employ.

**Don't bother with a built-in sandpit.** In the UK, they get really gross and uninviting very quickly. Cats love them if left uncovered (gag), and the shelf life of the kids using them is usually very brief. If you do install one, be sure it has a good cover on it for the reasons mentioned above.

**Sink the trampoline.** If you haven't bought one yet, sinking the trampoline into the ground is a game changer. You can still keep the net around it for safety, but sinking it instantly makes it less noticeable. Sinking it does mean you need to have it properly installed with appropriate drainage, of course.

Sinking the trampoline instantly makes it less of an eyesore and allows the opportunity for a more immersive play space.

**Paint the goals black or make them out of timber.** Bright, white plastic draws the eye. Or, if you can't do that or can't be bothered, then try to locate the goals further from the house and bring planting to the fore so they don't draw the eye.

**Try to screen the climbing frame.** This is easier in a larger garden, but even in a smaller one you can bring in trees or hedging just to soften the view and make it less of a focal point.

**Go natural.** There is something completely charming about an oak swing in a lovely old tree. It is utterly timeless and a toy for all ages, in my view, so where possible, choose natural materials such as timber for play, rather than plastic.

# FURNITURE

Furniture can make or break your garden. I am going to go full histrionic designer here and state that this is one of *the* most important elements of your space. I have seen many a beautiful garden that has been blighted by hideous furniture.

## Design guidelines

I am trusting you to forgive me for being so sassy, but you are reading a design book after all, and it's my job to be very clear about what makes good design, and what looks good and what doesn't. Now, this doesn't mean it needs to cost the earth. Here are a couple of pointers to bear in mind.

### Keep it natural

My preference, as with all things garden, is to keep it natural. I love timber furniture, and if stored correctly, it can last a very long time. Zinc-coated furniture is absolutely stunning too, as is powder-coated steel and aluminium when it's in a really slick, narrow format (not big chunky ones that look rather severe).

Of course, there can be tension between your desire for practicality versus aesthetic – many people will favour plastic-based furniture or hefty metal-based sofas because they're marketed as bulletproof in all weathers. But often, though not always, with that comes a chunkiness and lack of naturalness, which tends to leave me cold.

### Reflect your garden style

If you have a rustic or country-style garden, for example, then the furniture, like many other elements we have discussed, needs to reflect that style, so I would err towards timber or zinc-coated, which feels traditional and effortless.

If you have a more contemporary scheme, I would go for a modern take with clean-lined contemporary timber, which can soften and naturalize the space, slim-format, powder-coated steel, or rope-based furniture.

Timber furniture and neutral tones allow the furniture to blend into the landscape rather than compete with it.

## Choosing furniture

When you're choosing your furniture, ask yourself how many people you wish to seat, not only when it's just you and your household but also when you have guests, which will inform the size and amount of items you need. Of course, you need to choose your furniture based on the use of the space. If it's for dining, then a dining table and chairs are a given. If it's a space for relaxing or entertaining, then sofas and armchairs with a central coffee table or fire table are the way to go.

Think about what's going on inside your house too, and try to relate the furniture to your indoor furniture if you can – for example, if you have mid-century furniture inside, find something of a similar aesthetic for outside. You can have lots of fun with outdoor cushions to bring in a splash of colour too. I tend to steer clear of outdoor rugs, which can get pretty grotty in the UK climate. Be sure to buy some robust furniture covers for fleeting rain showers and winter storage if you can't store cushions under cover in winter.

Finally, for goodness sake, be sure to measure it all to make sure it fits. Refer to your scaled drawing so you can choose your furniture (or tweak your design) to fit what you want to include, and check back over the guide about negotiating around furniture in Chapter 3 (see p58).

# LIGHTING

Good lighting can elevate a space like nothing else. It's not a cheap element of the garden (what is?), but it's worth investing in. It can not only highlight features and focal points, but is also a useful wayfinding and security feature. It also eliminates the black mirror effect, where nighttime darkness is reflected back in the windows. The fittings need to be robust enough to withstand weather and any nibbling wildlife, so be sure to invest in the best fittings and electrician that you can.

## How much and where?

Now, I do not condone copious amounts of light. We are not lighting the garden up like Heathrow, and the less lighting we use the better to help support our beloved wildlife (see below). In fact, in some rural and conservation areas, lighting won't be allowed much, if at all, so do check with your local authority.

Lighting in gardens should have one or two purposes: either to highlight features and focal points or for wayfinding (or both). A beautiful effect can be to uplight architectural trees in the garden, particularly those with a decorative stem. Likewise, water features, pots, and sculpture can benefit from some gentle lighting to highlight their presence at night. Many people love a festoon light in a seating area to add a festive feel to a space.

For wayfinding, we want to avoid tripping over as we navigate around the garden at night. If possible, ensure there is lighting anywhere with level changes or steps. This can either be recessed in the step with light washing across the step to illuminate it, in a wall that envelopes the step, or in a bollard or spike to the side of the steps. Floodlights in the front or back garden can be good for the security conscious and to help navigate vehicles when arriving home in the dark.

## Keeping it wildlife friendly

We do want to limit light to where it is absolutely necessary. Any artificial light in a garden can disrupt the sleep/wake cycles of wildlife, so please make sure that any lighting you have is on a timer and not left on all night. Try to use downward-facing light, which is much kinder on wildlife and reduces upward glare, and opt for warmer hues with frosted glass, if possible.

## TOP TIPS FOR LIGHTING

**For colour temperature,** I always advise you use a warm white, which does as its name suggests – it's warming and inviting.

**Check the ingress protection** (IP) rating. The higher the IP, the more protection the light has from being outdoors in the elements. As a minimum, look for 65+ but do check with an electrician.

**Have more than one light circuit** so you have the flexibility to choose what is on and off at any one time, depending on how you are using the garden.

**Avoid uplighters in the ground** – they're going to glare straight in your eye. Save them for casting light up a tree, pot, or sculpture.

**If you have an outdoor kitchen,** you might consider installing some downlights so you can see what you are doing.

**A lot of your lighting won't be visible** if tucked into planting, so go for simple black fittings. For anything that's visible, you could complement the fittings in your house by using a bronze, chrome, or copper finish.

**Moonlighting** is a way of installing a light high in a tree to cast down (like moonlight) and can be very effective.

Lighting comes in a range of styles, from contemporary to rustic, to suit the style of your garden, and can be hidden away or made into a garden feature.

# SETTING IT ALL OUT

Now that you have your concept plan, and have chosen materials and finishes, you can draw them all in and create a setting-out plan, which is a plan with measurements on so you, or your builders, can accurately build the garden to the right size.

Mark your garden measurements with your scale ruler, and note down running measurements of all your key features such as paving, pathways, planting borders, and any other elements along the side of the plan. This will allow you to calculate square meterage of the materials you need, and also means you can grab yourself some spray marker and spray it out to see if it feels right to you too. If it doesn't feel quite right once you have calculated all your measurements, you can play around with it to get it to a size and shape you are happy with.

Make sure that stepping stones match your stride.

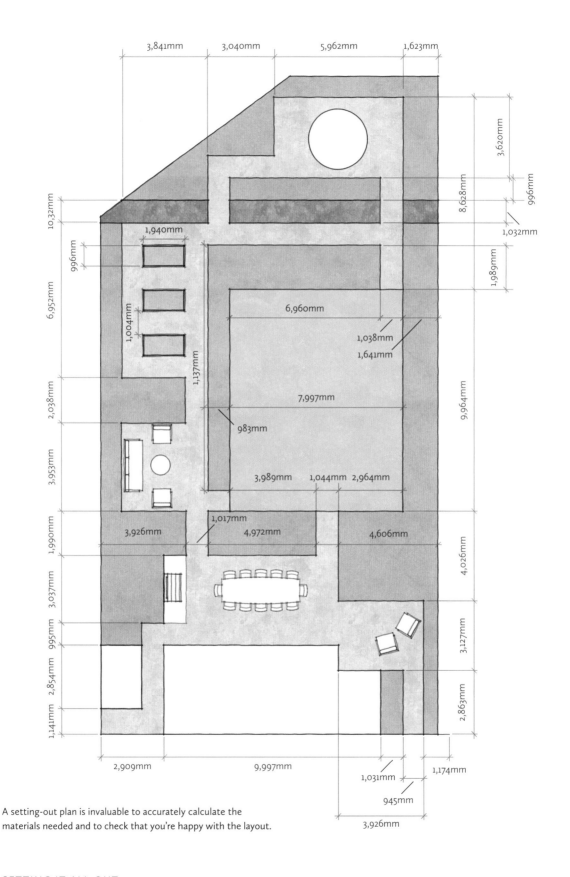

A setting-out plan is invaluable to accurately calculate the
materials needed and to check that you're happy with the layout.

SETTING IT ALL OUT

6

# PLANTING DESIGN

CHOOSING PLANTS, PLANTS FOR SEASONS AND PLACES,
YOUR PLANTING PLAN, AND PLANT RECIPES

Now that you've designed your garden, let's turn to planting
up those flowerbeds, or what we in the industry call borders.
It's time to select the plants you want to use.

# CHOOSING PLANTS

I know selecting plants can feel really overwhelming, but don't worry –
it's actually quite a methodical process when you know how. And let
me say right now, some of your choices will be wrong and some plants
will die. This is gardening. It's an art as well as a science, and even now,
plants fail in my garden – plants can be divas like that – but we can do
all the research necessary to mitigate this as much as possible.

When choosing your plants, we're going to consider the light, soil, and climate of
your garden; the purpose of the plants; planting style and setting; colour scheme;
seasonality; and size, shape, and habit. Let's look at each in turn.

## Light, soil, and climate

There is a famous saying by one of my favourite plantswomen/designers, Beth
Chatto: right plant, right place. In other words, you have to plant the right plants
in the right conditions or else they will fail. As we saw in Chapter 2 (see pp34–39),
different plants have different growing conditions, so the number one thing that
should influence your plant choice is the light and soil in your garden.

If you have a very shady garden, for instance, it's far better that we embrace
the shade-loving plants, accept that it's not going to be a colourful Mediterranean
garden, and instead spend the time picking out the very best shade/part-shade
plants for the space that will thrive. I've seen so many examples where people
ignore the lack of light in an area of the garden in the hope that sun lovers will
thrive, but trust me, it's a waste of your time and money. So take a copy of your
garden plan and jot down next to each border which are full sun and which are
part or full shade so that you can plan accordingly.

As a guide, if a plant is listed as needing full sun, it needs six or more hours of
sunlight a day. A part-shade plant needs three to six hours. Full shade is less than
three hours of sunlight. The number of hours is measured in midsummer, as all of
these areas will get fewer in winter when the sun is lower.

Likewise with soil – when choosing your plants, we'll filter them by their soil
needs, so just bear your soil type in mind as we start to make a list. When you choose
your plants, it's worth looking each one up online to check its soil and light needs.

Alliums (above) are marvellous bulbs for May and June colour. *Oenothera lindheimeri* 'Whirling Butterflies' (above right) provides wonderful movement in midsummer.

Your climate will also have a bearing on your plant selection. If you have a windy site, for instance, we need to pick wind-resilient options. Similarly, if you have a sun trap or frost pocket in your garden, we need to choose drought-resistant or hardy plants accordingly.

## Purpose

It may be that some of the planting in the garden is there to serve a purpose other than just being decorative – for example, you might want climbers or a hedge to screen off an unsightly shed, a multistem tree to act as a focal point, or a hedge to divide a space into different rooms, so bear in mind any plants that need to serve a purpose as you make your selections.

## Style and setting

Hopefully, when you put your moodboards together for the garden (see pp24–25), you included images of plants and/or planting schemes that you loved. Now refer back to them and make note of a few pointers. Is there a specific style or theme of planting that you have favoured? Is the planting romantic, formal, relaxed, informal, traditional, wild, coastal, and so on? And what about mood? Is it full of bold colour and shapes that are said to be energizing, or are there calm tones and fluffy textures, which bring a sense of tranquillity. Have you included images of a cottage garden, or are they more contemporary and minimalist? You don't need to know all the official styles, just take note of the general style of planting you like, which will help in selecting plants later.

It's also worth considering your setting. As a guide, when designing with plants, I keep the more "curated" elements of a scheme to the areas that are near the house. If you have a rural plot, for example, the goal is to blend the house and garden into the landscape, so as you move further from the house, planting should become looser and more naturalistic. A very formal planting mix in a field, for example, can look bizarre.

# COLOUR THEORY

Did you notice any colour theme? Now, the thing with colour schemes in the garden is you actually need several, as each season brings a different set of tones to the table to choose from. You can either stick with a palette that weaves through the seasons, or you can mix it up and have a scheme for spring, another for early summer, another for late summer, and so on – or something in between.

So, which colours are you drawn to? And which are you not so keen on? It's pretty common for clients to dislike yellow, orange, and red – and in large quantities, I can appreciate the point of view – but each colour has its place in different seasons. For example, I wouldn't be without the buttery yellows and fiery oranges of deciduous trees in autumn. Equally, pale yellow or vibrant orange can be a brilliant counterpoint to a sea of purple and bring a scheme together, and the rich late summer burnt oranges can look spectacular with ornamental grasses – so keep an open mind. Now let's dive into some colour theory so you can nail down the scheme(s) for your garden.

## COLOUR WHEEL

When choosing your colour combinations, it's worth considering the colour wheel and selecting from the styles opposite.

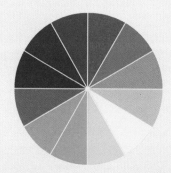

## Monochromatic

This is a scheme in which a range of shades and tones all come from the same colour – for example, a scheme of lilac, pale purple, deep purple, and mauve shades. This can be dramatic but arguably a little one note so use it with caution. Another example would be a palette of varying shades of green, which can be extremely elegant in a scheme if you like the restrained look.

## Analogous

These schemes are made up of colours that sit next to each other on the colour wheel, such as yellow, orange, and red, or purple and blue. Choosing analogous colours is a sure-fire way of creating a harmonious scheme, and depending on the mix of colours you choose, can create a really energetic or calming scheme that just feels right.

## Contrasting or complementary

These schemes pair colours from opposite sides of the colour wheel, such as blue and orange or purple and yellow. They can pack a real punch in a scheme, and you can play with the ratios if you want to keep it low key so that it's mostly one colour with a splash of the other, or go bolder with the split if you like. One of my favourites is a blue and purple scheme with a little splash of orange and pale yellow to add some depth – heaven.

## Triadic

These schemes use three colours that are evenly spaced around the colour wheel, such as blue or green, red or violet, and yellow. A triadic scheme can lead to a little more complexity, but you need to be careful with your ratios, as you don't necessarily want to use them all in equal proportions. Ideally, aim for a ratio of 6:3:1, with one dominant colour (60 per cent) and two accent colours at 30 per cent and 10 per cent.

You can use the colour wheel to create impactful planting in monochromatic, analogous, contrasting, or triadic schemes.

# Creating seasonal interest

Whenever I design a planting plan, my goal is to make sure that the planting scheme is bringing interest throughout the year, not just in midsummer. It's easy to get lured into planting a mass of the lovely and enticing summer-flowering perennials and shrubs, and forget to add in spring, autumn, and winter interest. So year-round interest is what we're going to focus on here.

## Make a spreadsheet

One of the best ways to make sure that you have plants for all seasons is to create a spreadsheet or list with the months of the year along the top, and the plants listed on the left. Colour in the months that the plant is in leaf in green, the months it's in flower in another brighter colour, and autumn interest such as seedheads or fading/brown/yellow leaves coloured in brown. You will see instantly where your gaps are and where you might need to swap some things out or add some in. You can also get really into it and colour code by flower colours per month to make sure you've got a harmonious mix – this is the joy of the spreadsheet.

## Embrace decay

Now, when thinking about seasonality, it's important that, if possible, you come around to a way of thinking that you may resist at first – and that's to embrace the beauty of decay. "Polly, I don't want dead-looking plants" is a common phrase from clients when we are talking autumn and winter interest, but it's just a matter of perspective. The faded brown seedheads of certain perennials can look incredible in the winter light, and offer food for birds, shelter for insects, and also, in my view, an infinitely more interesting scene than swathes of bare earth.

Likewise, the brown leaves of deciduous hedging such as *Carpinus* (hornbeam) or *Fagus* (beech) – these brilliant plants hold onto (most) of their leaves over the winter, so you have a beautiful brown silhouette of a hedge or topiarized shape, which I think looks utterly fabulous with the winter sun streaming through. The faded stalks of ornamental grasses swishing around in the breeze are also brilliant for interest, so be sure to include them in your spreadsheet for autumn and winter.

## Garden size and layout

The size and layout of your garden are really important. We spend much of our time indoors, particularly in winter, so we need to make sure that your direct views from the house, and those close to front and back doors and driveways, carry the principle of seasonal interest. This principle can be applied regardless of your garden size – if it's in sight from the house, drive, or main paths, make it seasonal and make it work hard for you. If it's not in main view, you have a little more wiggle room.

If you have a larger garden that isn't all visible from the house, for instance, or have areas that are tucked away, seasonality is less important, and it becomes more about making areas look their best at the times you will be using them. For example, we will often go for full-on summer planting around a concealed swimming pool, as, let's face it, that's when it's going to get the most use.

# Size, shape, and habit

It's so important when planning your planting scheme that you look at the eventual spread of each plant you are including. When we map out the plants, we draw them up by the size they will get to when mature (not the size they arrive as), so check the eventual spreads of the plants you are buying.

This is another reason why we draw the garden up to scale – it means we can map out the exact right number of plants. If something is going to take 20 years to reach its maximum size, we might allow a little more planting to fill the gaps while we wait. The same applies to anything that has the capacity to get large but that will be pruned to stay a certain size. As with all things garden, there are grey areas!

The actual form (or outline) of the plants is also important. We want to create a variety of different shapes in your border. You don't want all spiky plants or all domes – it's the mix of spikes, such as Culver's root (*Veronicastrum*) or iris; domes, such as geranium, *Nepeta*, or domed topiary; fans, such as ferns or grasses; and froth, such as fennel or meadow rue (*Thalictrum*), that makes for an interesting and textural scheme. So also note down the general shape of the plant – if you want to be really thorough, you can put them all on another spreadsheet to make sure you have a mix. Aim for 15–20 per cent spikes, 40 per cent mounds, 40 per cent fans, and maybe 5 per cent of froth.

Likewise with texture, plants can have different textural qualities, from fuzzy and frilly to smooth and sleek. Make sure you have a variety of textures to keep it interesting, such as the fuzzy fronds of a fern, the frilly leaves of an artemisia, and the smooth leaves of a hosta.

It's also worth bearing in mind the design principle of balance here – we don't want to have a garden with very tall things on one side and short on the other. So bear heights and scale of the plants in mind to make sure things feel relatively even. This doesn't mean you need to go matchy-matchy with symmetry – in fact, unless you are going very traditional, I would avoid it. They don't even have to be the same plant or the exact same height – it just needs to feel balanced.

Mix and match your textures for a more interesting scheme (below right). *Taxus* domes are a great example of a mound shape, while grasses form fan shapes (below).

## Maintenance

As we've seen, all gardens require maintenance, but plants can vary in their maintenance needs, from shrubs or grasses that need one prune a year, through to rather exhaustive staking, deadheading, and slug prevention for some of the more diva-ish perennials. In terms of maintenance, one prune a year is the least you can realistically aspire to achieve. Once planting is mature and bare earth covered to reduce weeding, arguably a lawn is higher maintenance than planting. Many perennials need not a lot more than a prune or two a year with some deadheading if you want to see more flowers over a longer season. If you want low maintenance, try to steer clear of anything that needs staking or multiple prunes a year, such as delphiniums or lots of roses.

## Layering

A good planting scheme is made up of a series of planting layers, and you can take inspiration from the planting you find in nature to see how this works. Take a woodland, for example: it consists of a tree canopy, a shrub understorey, and a ground layer. Your planting plan needs to therefore have a mix of bulbs, perennials, shrubs, and trees, each forming a different layer of the planting. In small spaces, this might be a single tree or a handful of shrubs; in larger spaces, far more. I'll always start with the upper layer – in other words, the placement of trees, followed by the mid-layer of shrubs, then the fillers of perennials and grasses, and finally, the bulbs.

You can also factor in layering in terms of heights. In typical borders that back onto a wall, fence, or hedge, we focus on the tallest at the back and a gradual decrease in height as we reach the front of the border – you need to give borders enough depth to accommodate this. In floating islands, or those with no "back", the height is in the centre. There are, of course, exceptions to this, such as where tall but ethereal and slimline plants weave through the border both front and back, so it depends a little on the heft of the plant as to where it sits.

## Repeat and cluster

One of the main reasons the planting schemes of the pros look so good is that they rely heavily on repetition. Repeating plants, or indeed repeating shapes, textures, or colours, gives a scheme a sense of cohesion and rhythm. You can do this in a number of ways:

**Repeating formal domes** of *Taxus* (yew), *Prunus lusitanica* (Portuguese laurel), *Pittosporum*, or any other clipped shapes in a border gives a very clear form that will endure through the seasons. This can instantly tie a scheme together.

**Herbaceous planting in groups looks better** when plants are positioned in odd numbers or multiples of three, such as three, five, six, or more. These clusters can

This deep border allows for layers of plants at different heights.

then be repeated down the border either in similar (but ideally not always identical) numbers. When we plant herbaceous perennials, it's very rare we plant them in singles unless they get large enough on their own (and by large enough, I mean about 80cm–1m/32–39in) that they don't need to be planted with friends. Again, it's about balance. A single *Geum* that is about 30cm (12in) at its maximum is going to look weird and spotty next to a big mound of geraniums or a shrub at 80cm (32in).

**Make sure your planting borders are deep** enough to allow for horizontal layers of plants. I've probably clobbered you with this enough by now, but allowing for deep borders means you can have two to three clusters in a row, front to back. The depth is what gives the wow factor.

## AVOIDING STRAIGHT LINES

Avoid straight lines! Unless it's a hedge or edging, you want to avoid lines of plants, and instead arrange in irregular drifts, diamonds, or triangles. You rarely find straight lines in nature.

In this urban space, an old apple tree was retained as it was still providing a bounty of apples each autumn and valuable screening for the left boundary. New multistem Tibetan cherry trees (*Prunus serrula*) were introduced into the heart of the garden for their ornamental value.

PLANTING DESIGN

# What if I don't have a blank canvas?

It's rare that you will have a garden that's completely devoid of plants at the start. You might have some shrubs or trees or even perennials already, so let's have a chat about this as it causes much angst.

I firmly believe that you have to love the plants in your garden. If you have some plants or shrubs in your garden that you love – great! They can either stay where they are if they work with the design, or if they aren't too mature, we can move them. This is best done when they are dormant in winter.

Now, I am also going to give you permission to remove any plants you hate. I am not saying remove the lot, and nor am I saying take down trees – wherever possible, we will preserve all trees – but in circumstances where they have to be removed for very legitimate reasons, from poor health to having outgrown the space, then we always replace with more than are taken away.

When it comes to other plants, I have had so many clients with horrible old overgrown shrubs or ratty orange roses that they feel too guilty to cull, and so put up with something that's not suitable or is overgrown or just plain ugly. Just because it's there doesn't mean you have to keep it. But nor does it mean you have to kill it – waste not want not – if you can and it's moveable, give it to a friend, school, community growing group, or pop it online for someone to come and give it a chance of a second life. If it's enormous and not moveable, then we need to consider if it has redeeming features, such as a lovely stem that we can reveal with some crown lifting, or if it can be pruned back to a more manageable shape.

# PLANTS FOR SEASONS AND PLACES

Now that you understand plant needs and planting design principles, we can start to look at the best plants for your garden. I've made lists of some of my favourite plants, first according to season and then by their location or use in the garden. I've divided them into layers – trees, shrubs, perennials, climbers, bulbs, and annuals and biennials – so that you can be sure to introduce variety and create interest. This list is by no means exhaustive, and there are so many more to choose from – it's simply a jumping-off point for some classics I love to use, so do go to the RHS website and sort by season, sunlight, or soil to see even more.

Let's start by looking at plants by season. That way, you can be sure to choose plants from each season to be sure you tick that seasonal interest box.

## Spring

### TREES

*Amelanchier lamarckii*
*Cercis siliquastrum*
*Cornus mas*
*Crataegus monogyna*
*Malus* 'Evereste'
*Prunus* 'Pink Perfection'
*Pyrus calleryana* 'Chanticleer'

### SHRUBS

*Camellia japonica* 'Nuccio's Cameo'
*Ceanothus* 'Concha'
*Chaenomeles speciosa* 'Geisha Girl'
*Daphne* x *transatlantica* PINK FRAGRANCE ('Blapink')
*Philadelphus* 'Belle Étoile'
*Ribes sanguineum* 'Elkington's White'
*Syringa* BLOOMERANG DARK PURPLE ('Smsjbp7')
*Viburnum opulus* 'Roseum'

### PERENNIALS

*Aquilegia vulgaris* var. *stellata* 'Black Barlow'
*Brunnera macrophylla* 'Mister Morse'
*Erysimum* 'Bowles's Mauve'
*Euphorbia characias* subsp. *wulfenii*
*Geum* 'Totally Tangerine'
*Lamprocapnos spectabilis* 'Alba'
*Lupinus* 'Masterpiece'
*Nepeta racemosa* 'Walker's Low'

### CLIMBERS

*Akebia quinata* cream-flowered
*Clematis armandi* (group 1)
*Clematis* x *cartmanii* 'Avalanche' (group 1)
*Clematis montana* var. *montana* (group 1)
*Wisteria sinensis* 'Prolific'

### BULBS

There are thousands and this is a near-impossible choice, but to name a few...
*Crocus* 'Jeanne d'Arc'
*Fritillaria meleagris*
*Hyacinthus orientalis* 'Woodstock'
*Muscari armeniacum*
*Narcissus* 'Thalia'
*Tulipa* 'Ballerina', 'Greenstar', 'Pink Star', 'Sarah Raven', 'White Triumphator'

### ANNUALS AND BIENNIALS

*Digitalis* × *mertonensis*
*Lunaria annua*

## Early summer

### TREES

*Cercis canadensis* 'Forest Pansy'
*Cornus controversa* 'Variegata'
*Cornus kousa* var. *chinensis*
*Cornus kousa* 'Miss Satomi'
*Davidia involucrata*
*Laburnum* × *watereri* 'Vossii'

### SHRUBS

*Choisya ternata*
*Cotinus* 'Grace'
*Deutzia* × *hybrida* 'Mont Rose'
*Lavandula angustifolia* 'Munstead'
*Rosa* DESDEMONA ('Auskindling')
*Rosa* OLIVIA ROSE AUSTIN
    ('Ausmixture')
*Rosa* ROALD DAHL ('Ausowlish')
*Salvia rosmarinus* 'Miss Jessopp's
    Upright'
*Weigela* ALL SUMMER PEACH
    ('Slingpink')

### PERENNIALS

*Astrantia major* 'Star of Billion'
*Astrantia* 'Roma'
*Cirsium rivulare* 'Atropurpureum'
*Geranium* ROZANNE ('Gerwat')
*Iris* 'Jane Phillips'
*Oenothera lindheimeri* 'Whirling
    Butterflies'
*Paeonia lactiflora* 'Coral Charm'
*Salvia nemorosa* 'Caradonna'
*Veronicastrum virginicum*
    'Fascination'

### CLIMBERS

*Actinidia kolomikta*
*Clematis purpurea* 'The President'
    (group 2)
*Jasminum officinale* 'Devon
    Cream'
*Rosa* THE GENEROUS GARDENER
    ('Ausdrawn')

*Rosa* THE LADY OF THE LAKE
    ('Ausherbert')
*Trachelospermum jasminoides*

### BULBS

*Allium hollandicum* 'Purple
    Sensation'
*Allium* 'Purple Rain', 'Silver Spring'
*Allium siculum*
*Allium stipitatum* 'Mount Everest'
*Gladiolus communis* subsp.
    *byzantinus*
*Lilium* 'Claude Shride'

### ANNUALS AND
### BIENNIALS

*Antirrhinum majus* 'Appleblossom'
*Cerinthe major* 'Purpurascens'
*Eschscholzia californica* 'Ivory
    Castle'
*Lathyrus odoratus* 'Matucana'
*Linaria maroccana*

## Late summer

### TREES

*Heptacodium miconioides**

### SHRUBS

*Buddleja davidii* 'Black Knight'
*Euonymus europaeus* 'Red
    Cascade'
*Hydrangea arborescens* STRONG
    ANNABELLE ('Abetwo')
*Leycesteria formosa* 'Purple Rain'
*Veronica* 'Autumn Glory'

### PERENNIALS

*Agastache* 'Blackadder'
*Anemone* × *hybrida*
    'Honorine Jobert'
*Coreopsis verticillata* 'Moonbeam'
*Echinacea purpurea*
*Helenium* 'Moerheim Beauty'
*Hylotelephium spectabile* (Brilliant
    Group) 'Brilliant'
*Salvia* 'Amistad'
*Verbena bonariensis*

### CLIMBERS

*Campsis* × *tagliabuana* 'Madame
    Galen'
*Clematis* 'Étoile Violette' (group 3)
*Lonicera periclymenum* 'Serotina'

### BULBS

*Allium* 'Millennium'
*Crocosmia* × *crocosmiiflora* 'Emily
    McKenzie'
*Dahlia* 'Totally Tangerine', 'Verrone's
    Obsidian', 'Wine Eyed Jill'
*Galtonia candicans*
*Gladiolus murielae*

### ANNUALS AND
### BIENNIALS

*Amaranthus caudatus*
*Cleome houtteana* 'Helen Campbell'
*Cobaea scandens*
*Cosmos bipinnatus* 'Purity'
*Ipomoea purpurea* 'Grandpa Otts'

\* Classed as a shrub but can
be grown as a small tree.

## Autumn

### TREES

Acer palmatum 'Dissectum'*
Cercidiphyllum japonicum
Ginkgo biloba
Liquidambar styraciflua
Parrotia persica

### SHRUBS

Arbutus unedo
Callicarpa bodinieri var. giraldii
  'Profusion'
Cotinus coggygria 'Royal Purple'
Hydrangea quercifolia
Physocarpus 'Amber Jubilee'
Rhus typhina

\* Classed as a shrub but can
be grown as a small tree.

### PERENNIALS

Anemone x hybrida 'Honorine
  Jobert'
Aster x frikartii 'Mönch'
Liriope muscari
Penstemon 'Raven'
Rudbeckia fulgida var. sullivantii
  'Goldsturm'

### CLIMBERS

Ampelopsis brevipedunculata
Parthenocissus tricuspidata
  'Veitchii'
Vitis vinifera 'Purpurea'

### BULBS

Colchicum autumnale 'Album'
Colchicum 'Waterlily'
Cyclamen hederifolium var.
  hederifolium f. albiflorum
Galanthus reginae-olgae subsp.
  reginae-olgae
Nerine bowdenii 'Ella K'
Sternbergia lutea

### ANNUALS AND BIENNIALS

Rhodochiton atrosanguineus
Zinnia 'Queeny Lime Red'

Note: Most late summer annuals
will happily carry on into autumn.

## Winter

### TREES

Acacia dealbata
Acer griseum
Betula utilis subsp. jacquemontii
Hamamelis x intermedia*
Taxus baccata

### SHRUBS

Cornus sanguinea 'Midwinter Fire'
Daphne bholua 'Jacqueline Postill'
Edgeworthia chrysantha
Sarcococca confusa
Viburnum x bodnantense 'Dawn'

\* Classed as a shrub but can
be grown as a small tree.

### PERENNIALS

Bergenia 'Bressingham White'
Helleborus × hybridus Harvington
  white speckled
Iris unguicularis
Viola odorata

### CLIMBER

Clematis cirrhosa var.
  purpurascens 'Freckles' (group 1)

### BULBS

Eranthis hyemalis
Galanthus nivalis

# Plants for places

Now we've covered some favourites, let's take a look at some plants for specific places, because as you now know, it's not just about what looks good, plants also need to work in the conditions you have.

## HEDGING PLANTS

*Carpinus betulus* (deciduous)
*Crataegus monogyna* (deciduous)
*Euonymus japonicus* 'Jean Hugues' (evergreen)
*Fagus sylvatica* (deciduous)
*Ilex aquifolium* (evergreen)
*Prunus lusitanica* (evergreen)
*Taxus baccata* (evergreen)

## ORNAMENTAL GRASSES

Much like bulbs, there are hundreds to choose from, and these are just a few favourites.

*Deschampsia cespitosa* 'Goldtau'
*Hakonechloa macra*
*Melica altissima* 'Alba'
*Miscanthus sinensis* 'Gracillimus'
*Pennisetum* 'Fairy Tails'
*Seslaria autumnalis*
*Stipa gigantea*
*Stipa tenuissima*

## PLANTS FOR SHADE

*Bistorta officinalis* 'Superba'
*Brunnera macrophylla* 'Jack Frost'
*Epimedium* x *youngianum* 'Niveum'
*Geranium phaeum*
*Polystichum setiferum*
*Veronicastrum virginicum* 'Fascination'
*Vinca minor*

## COASTAL PLANTS

*Armeria maritima* 'Morning Star White'
*Artemisia* 'Powis Castle'
*Eryngium* x *zabelii* 'Neptune's Gold'
*Euonymus japonicus*
*Pinus nigra*
*Santolina chamaecyparissus*

## PLANTS FOR DAMP CONDITIONS

*Iris sibirica*
*Lamprocapnos spectabilis* 'Alba'
*Leycesteria formosa* 'Purple Rain'
*Osmunda regalis*
*Primula japonica* 'Miller's Crimson'
*Sanguisorba officinalis*
*Trollius europaeus*

## PLANTS FOR GRAVEL GARDENS

*Achillea* 'Credo'
*Erigeron karvinskianus*
*Euphorbia characias* 'Silver Swan'
*Lavandula angustifolia* 'Hidcote'
*Phlomoides tuberosa* 'Amazone'
*Pseudodictamnus mediterraneus*
*Salvia* 'Blue Spire'
*Salvia rosmarinus*
*Santolina chamaecyparissus*
*Stachys byzantina* 'Big Ears'
*Thymus vulgaris*

## ROCKERY PLANTS

*Aubrieta* 'Purple Cascade'
*Campanula carpatica* 'Blaue Clips'
*Festuca glauca*
*Iberis* 'Masterpiece'
*Isotoma fluviatilis*
*Juniperus horizontalis* or *J. communis* 'Repanda'
*Phlox subulata* 'Snowflake'
*Pinus mugo* 'Mops'
*Thymus serpyllum*

## CONTAINER PLANTS

*Agapanthus* POPPIN' PURPLE ('Mp003')
*Nemesia* 'Wisley Vanilla'
*Pelargonium* 'Attar of Roses'
*Petunia* 'Tidal Wave Silver'
*Pittosporum tobira* 'Nanum'
*Primula auricula* 'Black Jack'
*Prunus lusitanica*
*Skimmia* 'Kew Green'
*Taxus baccata*

## PLANTS FOR A BALCONY OR ROOF TERRACE

*Alchemilla mollis*
*Agapanthus* 'Black Pantha'
*Buddleja* 'Pink Delight'
*Calamagrostis* x *acutiflora* 'Karl Foerster'
*Euphorbia* × *martini*
*Lavandula angustifolia* 'Munstead'
*Phillyrea angustifolia*
*Pinus mugo*
*Prunus lusitanica* 'Angustifolia'
*Salvia* 'Nachtvlinder'
*Salvia nemorosa* 'Caradonna'
*Salvia rosmarinus*
*Trachelospermum jasminoides*

Planting borders are oversized and generous to provide a dramatic view both from the house and the upper terrace. The width and mass also balances out the void of the adjacent lawn.

Sawn limestone paving continues the contemporary theme, complementing the buff tones of the house.

A crisp mown lawn contrasts with the softer wildflowers and surrounding borders, creating a pleasing contrast between formal and informal.

Planting was used to blur the boundary between the formal garden and fields beyond. Post-and-rail fencing keeps grazing animals out of the garden without blocking the view.

# YOUR PLANTING PLAN

Hopefully, now you have put together a list of plants that you want to use in your garden based on the plants I have recommended or that you have researched. You have checked the soil and light needs, and know that the plants you have chosen are suitable for your particular garden. Your list should include trees, shrubs, perennials, grasses, and bulbs.

Chances are you have too many. The art of a good planting scheme is restraint – fewer plants repeated is going to look better than loads of plants barely repeated, which can feel disjointed and spotty. Of course, if you have an enormous garden, you are going to need more than if you have an urban garden – but still, go back and edit it. I'm going to show you some plans later (see pp152–55), and you'll see the list is more limited than you might think.

Once you have your plan, you can tot up the numbers of each plant ready for ordering or growing. I don't tend to mark bulbs on as I'd be marking hundreds of tiny dots – not good. So, instead, spend some time thinking about a mix per planting area and just jot it down next to the relevant border. For example, you might have a "by-the-house mix" of tulips, narcissus, and alliums. In the lawn, you may have a more informal mix such as narcissus, crocus, fritillary, and camassia. Be careful to pay attention to your sunlight when choosing the bulbs – most, but not all, need full sun.

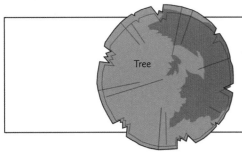

1. So where do we start? With structure, of course – always structure. Take a copy of your concept plan, or a fresh sheet of tracing paper overlaid on your concept plan, and mark on your chosen trees. When positioning trees, think about their function. Are they to screen, act as a focal point, or provide shade or height? No garden should be without at least one tree – even very compact ones – it's just about finding the right tree for your garden.

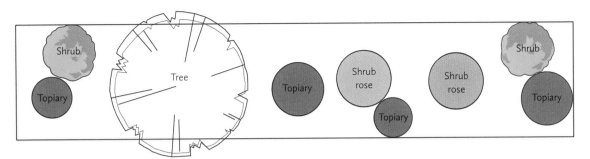

2. Next, mark out your structural planting. This is likely going to be your hedges, shrubs, and evergreens. Often this is topiary domes or chunky evergreen mounds, but not always. Remember when marking these on the plan to draw them at the size they will grow to (or that you plan to keep them to), and also consider their height so you get the position right. You don't want a tall shrub at the front of the border. You also don't want to overcrowd your border, so double-check online what the spread is and mark it on the plan.

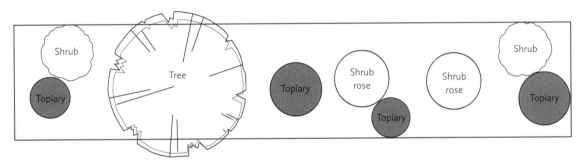

3. Be sure to repeat your structural planting around the garden to give that pacing and rhythm we talked about earlier (see p140) – here, the topiary domes are repeated down the border.

You should now have the start of a pattern in the planting where the eye scans from one plant to the next.

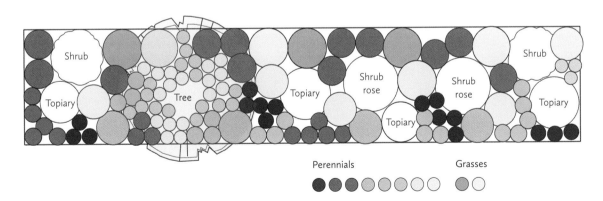

Perennials                                          Grasses

4. Now we can add the perennials and grasses. Remember to follow the repeat and cluster rules mentioned earlier – you want to create drifts of plants that merge into each other and are in irregular shapes. Place the taller grasses and perennials at the back and the shorter ones at the front so that the height graduates down, but it's no bad thing if it's a little variable – nature isn't uniform. Note that annuals and biennials are added to the plan annually.

# PLANT RECIPES

I know that choosing the right mix of plants can be daunting, even with the information above, so I have curated some plant recipes for you that you can copy if you so wish (and have the appropriate conditions), or you can get your eye into the mix and then swap things out for your preferred plants. You'll see there is a variety of trees, shrubs, and perennials, which span the seasons and vary in height and texture.

## Recipe for a sunny border (all seasons)

### TREE
○ *Malus* 'Evereste'

### TOPIARY
● *Taxus baccata* (50cm/20in ball)

### SHRUB
◐ *Rosa* OLIVIA ROSE AUSTIN ('Ausmixture')

### PERENNIALS
● *Agastache* 'Blackadder'
○ *Alchemilla mollis*
● *Astrantia* 'Roma'
○ *Echinacea purpurea* 'Alba'
◐ *Euphorbia characias* subsp. *characias* 'Humpty Dumpty'
● *Geranium* 'Azure Rush'
● *Hylotelephium* 'Matrona'
○ *Oenothera lindheimeri* 'Whirling Butterflies'
● *Salvia nemorosa* 'Caradonna'

### ORNAMENTAL GRASSES
○ *Miscanthus sinensis* 'Gracillimus'
◐ *Pennisetum* 'Fairy Tails'

### CLIMBER
○ *Trachelospermum jasminoides*

### BULB
● *Iris* 'Jane Phillips'

*Hylotelephium* 'Matrona'

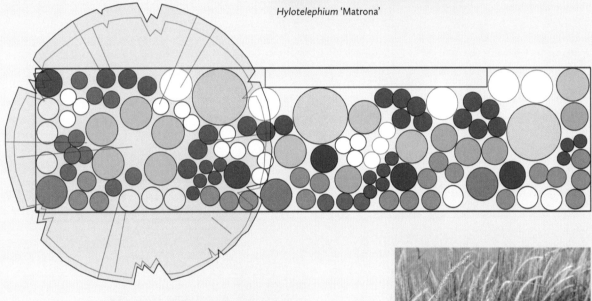

*Pennisetum* 'Fairy Tails'

*Oenothera lindheimeri* 'Whirling Butterflies'

# Recipe for a part-shade border (all seasons)

**TREE**

◯ *Cornus kousa* var. *chinensis* 'China Girl'

**TOPIARY**

● *Taxus baccata* (50cm/20in and 70cm/28in balls)

**SHRUB**

◯ *Hydrangea paniculata* 'Limelight'

**PERENNIALS**

◯ *Anemone* x *hybrida* 'Honorine Jobert'

● *Astrantia* 'Roma'

◯ *Brunnera macrophylla* 'Jack Frost'

◯ *Digitalis* x *mertonensis*

◯ *Geranium sanguineum* var. *striatum*

◯ *Helleborus* x *hybridus* Harvington double white

◯ *Sanguisorba officinalis*

**ORNAMENTAL GRASS**

◯ *Hakonechloa macra*

**FERN**

◯ *Blechnum spicant*

**CLIMBER**

◯ *Clematis montana* var. *grandiflora* (group 1)

*Brunnera macrophylla* 'Jack Frost'

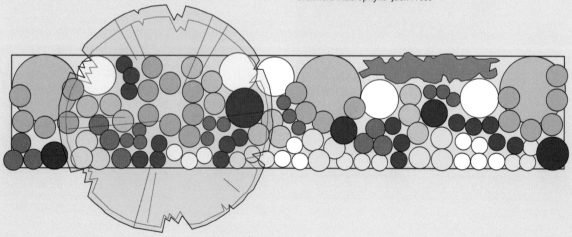

# Recipe for a shade border (all seasons)

### SHRUBS

- ○ *Osmanthus x burkwoodii*
- ● *Sarcococca confusa*
- ○ *Viburnum x bodnantense* 'Dawn'
- ● *Vinca minor*

### PERENNIALS

- ○ *Anemone × hybrida* 'Honorine Jobert
- ○ *Bistorta officinalis* 'Superba'
- ○ *Brunnera macrophylla* 'Jack Frost'
- ○ *Epimedium x youngianum* 'Niveum'
- ● *Euphorbia amygdaloides* var. *robbiae*
- ● *Geranium phaeum*
- ○ *Helleborus niger*
- ○ *Lamprocapnos spectabilis* 'Alba'
- ○ *Liriope muscari*

### FERN

- ● *Polystichum setiferum*

### CLIMBER

- ○ *Clematis cirrhosa* 'Freckles' (group 1)

*Geranium phaeum*

*Clematis cirrhosa* 'Freckles'

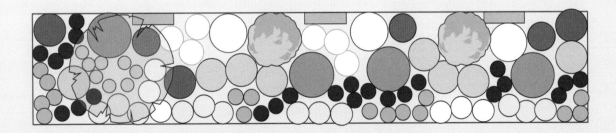

# BEFORE YOU PLANT

There are a few things to consider before you go putting all those lovely plants into the garden, including plant sizes to buy, the best time to plant during the growing year, preparing your soil for optimum growing conditions, and how to give your brand-new plants the best chance to thrive.

## Buying your plants

Trees and plants are supplied in different sizes, and the larger the tree/plant, the higher the price. When buying trees, you order them by their height and also by the girth of the trunk (the larger the girth, the more mature the tree). This is when buying trees online can be problematic, as you may order a tree thinking you are getting the lovely mature tree in the photo, only to realize you are getting a far younger version of said tree and you will need to wait rather a while for it to do its thing. Do check to see if the tree in the image is the actual size you are getting. Or even better if you can, go and pick it out yourself – I've included some great suppliers at the back (see p186).

With perennials and shrubs in pots, you can buy in various pot sizes from the smallest, 9cm (3½in), up to 10, 15, and 20 litres (2, 3, and 4 gallons) and more. Shrubs are often slower growers, so I recommend you buy them in the biggest pot size your budget can stretch to. For perennials, I tend to buy 2-litre (2-quart) pots because they give impact within the first year, but if you want to save money, you can buy in 9cm (3½in) pots and just be patient – they'll catch up within a year or two.

## When is the best time to plant?

The best time to plant a garden is between autumn and spring, just as long as the soil isn't frozen or waterlogged. It's also the best time to order trees and shrubs as autumn marks the start of root-ball season, when trees and shrubs are dug from the ground ready to be sold. There is a misconception among the general public that the best time to plant a garden is in summer – perhaps as that's when people care most about their garden – but it's actually the very worst time. Plants are in full-on growth mode, and so root disruption can shock them, resulting in sulking or, worse, failing plants. Better to do it as they are going to sleep in autumn or waking up in spring.

When setting out a new border, I always position all the plants in their pots before planting to check I'm happy with the composition.

## Preparing your soil and planting

By now, you should know how important your soil is for the success of your garden, so let's make sure it's at its best ready for planting. I am ashamed to say that in my early days of gardening (well before I studied it or worked in it, I hasten to add), I would just grab a trowel, scratch out the suggestion of a hole for whatever plant I had selected from the supermarket or garden centre, chuck it in, and backfill it with whatever knackered earth was surrounding it, usually with at least a couple of centimetres of the plant still proud of the ground. In hindsight, my soil was a hideous mix of compacted, flinty clay – it's a wonder anything grew.

So first up, be sure there is no compaction by turning over the soil with a fork, and then be sure it's well prepared by adding in plenty of organic matter in the form of well-rotted manure, garden compost, or mushroom compost. This is going to improve your soil whatever composition it is, so order yourself some tonne bags

Mulching will help to suppress weeds until the border fills out. Here, mature planting has reduced the space for weeds to grow.

of organic matter online and get that goodness into your soil – you want at least 5–10cm (2–4in) of organic matter added to the top and then turned into the existing soil. At this point, digging the holes for your plants should be easy as the soil will have been turned over and be nicely aerated. Hopefully it goes without saying, but be sure the soil isn't waterlogged before planting too.

Now dig a hole about twice the size of the plant you are going to plant. In the case of perennials, about 50 per cent bigger is fine. Remove your plant from its pot carefully, place it in the hole, and backfill with a mix of compost and your existing soil. Be sure the plant is level with the ground, not sitting proud or sunk below the surface. Firm the plant in to be sure that it's not got any big air pockets and that it's surrounded with soil, and water well.

## Mulch

After you have finished planting, it's a good idea to mulch a border, which just means adding a layer of well-rotted manure, mushroom compost, or fine bark chips to the top of the soil (being sure not to cover the plants). Not only does it finish it off beautifully from an aesthetic point of view, it also adds nutrients to the soil, suppresses weeds, and retains moisture.

---

## WATERING TIPS

Your goal with watering is to get water to the roots, not the surface. Here are some tips to make that happen:

- A great way to water trees is to install a pipe in the planting hole with the end of the piping poking above the soil level. This allows you to water directly to the root zone, which is where it is needed.
- To avoid a lot of surface runoff, create a raised ring of soil like a doughnut around any new plants and water inside. The water can't escape and has to move down through the soil, rather than run off the surface.
- Avoid watering in the middle of the day – it's best done in the early morning or in the evening when evaporation is less of an issue.
- Long and deep watering less often is better than a little and often, which encourages shallow roots.
- Install water butts on downpipes to collect rainwater, or if you are doing extensive buildworks, consider rainwater-harvesting tanks, which can feed drip irrigation systems.

# 7

# MONTH-BY-
MONTH
MAINTENANCE

## GARDEN TASKS FOR EVERY MONTH OF THE YEAR

In this chapter, you'll find a guide of what you need to be doing
in the garden each month. As with all things gardening, these
are suggestions rather than rules. The weather will dictate some
of the tasks and some jobs span more than one month. The one
exception is weeding, which needs to be done practically every
month. Here I've focused more on ornamental planting rather
than fruit and veg, which require a whole book of their own.

# JANUARY

It's January; the shortest day is behind us and it's time to emerge from those strange Betwixmas days and get in the garden. It may look a little bleak out there, but there are hints of spring on the horizon from the brave little snowdrops. January is a big pruning month, so sharpen those secateurs and grab your pruning saw – we have wisteria, roses, and deciduous trees to tame. And for those more partial to some armchair gardening, now's a great time to get browsing those seed catalogues ready for sowing in a month or two.

## TASKS THIS MONTH

- Clean and sharpen tools
- Sweep leaves and debris from paths and paving
- Fill bird feeders and birdbaths
- Order dahlias tubers ready to plant in March
- Order annual seeds such as *Cobaea*, *Ammi*, scabious, and *Nicotiana*
- Prune wisteria, roses, and apple and pear trees
- Plant bare-root/root-ball plants
- Cut back collapsed or mushy perennials
- Sow sweet peas (if you've not done so already)
- Cut off all old hellebore leaves at the first signs of new growth
- Take note of your winter structure

## Pruning

**Wisteria** January is the time to prune your wisteria prior to the growing season and to showcase the flowers in May. If you don't, you're going to have a whole lot of leaves and not as many flowers. Cut back the lateral stems you pruned in summer (trusting you did, but even if you didn't) to two or three buds. Be sure to cut just after a bud.

**Roses** Start with any dead, diseased, or damaged stems, and always cut to just above a bud. For climbing roses, prune sideshoots back to four healthy buds. For established shrub roses, cut back by one-third to keep the same size, cut back by half or more if you want to reduce the size, or cut back by less than a third if you want it taller. Pick up any fallen leaves to reduce the spread of the disease black spot. Roses are tough old birds, so don't be scared of them.

**Apple and pear trees** Remove dead, diseased, or damaged branches and remove any congested branches to open up the framework and allow more airflow.

## Plant bare-root/root-ball plants

There's still time! Bare-root and root-ball plants are cheaper than pot grown and are dug straight from the field and sent directly to you, usually arriving in a sack or as exposed root balls. Bare-root season tends to end in early March, so get ordering and plant as long as the ground isn't frozen or waterlogged. Wait for the spring for evergreens.

## Cut back collapsed or mushy perennials

It's around this time that some of the perennials you have left for winter interest start to look like a scraggly, mushy mess, so cut back and compost anything that ticks that box. Don't go hacking everything else back – it's still providing shelter for insects, and be sure to leave the ornamental grasses for now too. Just a note on composting: avoid composting diseased plants or weeds that have gone to seed as you don't want to see them return in years to come when you spread your compost.

## Winter structure

Take note of your winter structure – do you have enough? Is there a good proportion of evergreens for interest? If not, now's a good time to order more and plant in spring, as long as the soil isn't frozen or waterlogged.

Hydrangea seedheads create beautiful winter interest, particularly when they are dusted with frost.

# FEBRUARY

This might be my least favourite month in the garden, but thankfully, it's mercifully short and there are cheering signs of life from snowdrops, *Iris reticulata*, and crocuses. For those counting those daylight hours, Valentine's Day (14 February) stands as a beacon of hope, with 10 hours of sunlight in the UK, so light levels are rapidly increasing and seed sowing (for those inclined) is almost a goer.

## TASKS THIS MONTH

- Cut back deciduous ornamental grasses
- Sow tomatoes, chillies, and *Cobaea scandens*
- Improve your soil
- Prune clematis from groups 2 and 3
- Order annual seeds
- Water pots if the weather is dry
- Plant snowdrops in the green or divide congested clumps
- Fill bird feeders and birdbaths
- Mulch the garden before it gets too crowded

## Deciduous ornamental grasses

You can now cut down any deciduous ornamental grasses that were left standing over winter, including miscanthus, *Calamagrostis*, and *Hakonechloa*. Cut the entire clump back to a few centimetres from ground level and new shoots will soon appear. For evergreen grasses, such as various *Carex*, you need do very little other than remove any dead leaves in spring.

## Seed sowing

Starting seed sowing too soon runs the risk of leggy seedlings, and let's face it, it's a long time to nurture them indoors until the frosts pass. That said, now is a good time to sow tomatoes and chillies in a heated propagator or greenhouse or on a warm, sunny windowsill. If you are itching to get going with the flowers, you can also start to sow *Cobaea scandens* too. Don't sow the whole packet or you are going to be nurturing a veritable army of plants in spring.

## Improve your soil

Glamorous, it is not, but now is a great time to mulch borders and improve the soil by adding in some well-rotted manure or mushroom compost before it all gets too crowded and fiddly to do. Roses love well-rotted manure, so spread a good layer around them too.

## Prune clematis

Group 1 clematis flower in winter or early spring – leave them alone! Group 2 clematis flower in May/June and group 3 flower in July/August. These both need pruning now. For group 2, just work back from the end of each stem until you find a healthy bud. Snip above it and repeat across the plant. Group 3 need hard pruning, so be brave – cut them all the way down to the first healthy bud, which is usually 30cm (12in) from ground level. If in doubt, leave them alone and watch them this year so you know what to do next year.

## Water your pots

Watering pots might sound insane in midwinter, but tulips need water about eight weeks before they bloom to ensure healthy, tall stems, so keep an eye on the moisture levels of your pots to ensure you don't end up with stumpy tulips.

## Snowdrops

Plant snowdrops in the green or divide congested clumps. "In the green" means exactly that – snowdrops that have their leaves attached. These are much easier to establish than bulbs, so order them now or divide clumps that you already have.

Snowdrops are the perfect bulb to add cheer on wintry days.

# MARCH

March is such an enormous sigh of relief for me – the clocks soon go forward, the days are getting longer, and there is more to keep me amused in the garden. It's a month where the secateurs get a good workout and I get sowing annuals in earnest.

## TASKS THIS MONTH

- Deadhead spent daffodils and other spring bulbs
- Cut back any remaining perennials
- Prune deciduous shrubs such as buddleja, *Cornus*, and *Cotinus*
- Pot up dahlias
- Cut back tatty fern fronds
- Sow hardy and half-hardy annuals under cover
- Pinch out sweet pea tips to encourage bushy growth
- Plant summer-flowering bulbs such as gladioli, crocosmia, and lilies
- Lightly prune any straggly or frost-damaged lavender

## Deadhead spring bulbs

Deadheading spring bulbs allows for the energy to go back into the bulbs rather than on setting seed. Snip off the heads of spent flowers but leave the leaves intact to absorb all that sunlight goodness for next year.

## Cut back perennials and grasses

You can now cut back any remaining perennials and deciduous grasses that you left over the winter, as well as tired and tatty fern fronds. This makes way for the new growth and gets the garden primed and ready for the new season.

## Prune deciduous shrubs

Now is the perfect time to prune deciduous shrubs such as *Cornus*, *Cotinus*, and buddleja, which can be cut back hard now to encourage strong, bushy growth. Pruning deciduous shrubs in March helps to shape them, remove dead or diseased wood, and promote vigorous new growth. In the UK, the timing and type of pruning may differ slightly based on the local climate and plant species. Don't prune spring-flowering shrubs such as lilac and weigela, as these flower on last year's growth and are best pruned immediately after flowering.

Deadheading spring bulbs
ensures energy goes to the
bulb, not to setting seed.

## Pot up dahlia tubers

Hopefully, you ordered tubers earlier in the year
and it's now time to get them started. Plant them
individually in a 2–3-litre (2–3-quart) pot with the old
stem poking above the soil and the tubers below the
soil surface. Keep them somewhere frost free such
as a windowsill or greenhouse. If you have lots, you
can start them in large trays rather than pots. Make
sure the compost is moist but not sodden, and
continue to water when you see signs of life.

## Sow hardy and half-hardy annuals under cover

Sow annual seeds such as cosmos, *Ammi*, scabious,
and so many more, and keep them in a greenhouse
or on a sunny windowsill. Try to resist sowing the
entire pack unless you have an enormous garden –
you won't need that many and you'll find yourself
raising a menagerie of seedlings in April, which all
require potting on and greenhouse/windowsill space.

# APRIL

April can be fickle and unpredictable, but the days are longer, which can only mean one thing – more time to spend in the garden. It's a busy month as the soil warms up and you can almost feel the energy in the air. Any seedlings you have sown under cover should be coming along nicely, and soon annuals can be sown directly outdoors to fill the gaps in your borders. Cosmos, scabious, and poppies are great to weave through your perennial borders.

## TASKS THIS MONTH

- In milder areas, plant out tubers, corms, and rhizomes towards the end of the month when frosts have gone
- Continue to deadhead spent spring bulbs
- Prune hydrangeas
- Lift and divide summer-flowering perennials
- Protect plants from slugs and snails
- Increase watering and feeding of houseplants
- Prick out and pot on annual seedlings

## Plant out tubers, corms, and rhizomes

Towards the end of the month in milder areas, where the risk of frost has passed, you can plant out dahlia tubers (new ones and any you started in March), and stagger-plant gladioli corms to prolong the flowering period. Some will need support to train early growth, so clean up supports ready for use. Canna and agapanthus rhizomes can also be planted out in sunny spots.

## Spring bulb care

When spring bulbs such as narcissus and tulips finish flowering, be sure to deadhead them but leave the leaves alone. While they can look messy, the leaves of bulbs are like solar panels and the bulb is like a battery. The leaves need to be left intact to absorb sunlight to store energy. For pots you are keen to replant, you can always remove the bulbs (leaves intact) and relocate them to a quiet spot to die back out of sight. Any indoor bulbs can also be planted into borders.

Tulips can be either early or late varieties, so be sure to introduce both in your planting schemes.

## Prune hydrangeas

April is the perfect time to prune your beloved hydrangeas. For *H. arborescens* and *paniculata* varieties, cut about 20–30cm (8–12in) from ground level above the first healthy set of buds. This will ensure strong stems for summer. For mophead and lacecap varieties, you just need to deadhead the old flowers where they meet new growth and remove a third of the very old stems to allow good airflow.

## Lift and divide perennials

Lifting and dividing summer-flowering perennials will help to keep plants healthy and vigorous and gives you a great opportunity to multiply plants. Lift plants by digging them up, and divide them either by pulling them apart (for smaller plants) or using a spade to stomp through larger forms. You can also use two forks back to back as a lever, or even an old bread knife for the really tough ones. Replant and water well. Examples of good dividers include geraniums, ornamental grasses, asters, and phlox, but the list is far longer, so do your homework!

## Slug and snail patrol

As tender new shoots start to appear, so do the slugs and snails, which can't resist them. It's hard to say whether any of these are effective, but you could try protecting plants with protective barriers such as crushed shells, wool pellets, grit, and copper rings, or you could try biological control with nematodes. Alternatively, you could go on patrol with a torch at night and remove slugs and snails from your plants, but I'll leave that to you.

## Pot on annual seedlings

When seedlings develop their true leaves (rather than the first two that appear), prick them out and pot them into individual 9cm (3½in) pots. Gently loosen the soil before pricking the seedlings out and pull from the leaves to avoid crushing the stem. Be sure the entire root comes up with it – it won't survive without roots. Label and water.

# MAY

May is possibly my favourite time of the gardening year, with months of warm weather, light evenings, and abundant blooms stretching ahead of us. It's finally warm enough to direct-sow seedlings in the ground, and get those dahlias and seedlings hardened off and planted. RHS Chelsea Flower Show approaches in late May, and gardens are front of mind for many. By now, your garden should be filling out nicely, and the tulips should be handing over to the alliums for the next wave of bulb-based colour.

## TASKS THIS MONTH

- Harden off seedlings
- Continue to plant out dahlias
- No Mow May
- Chelsea chop
- Leave your spring bulbs to fade
- Tie in sweet peas
- Stake emerging plants that need support
- Feed and water pots and houseplants
- Prune spring-flowering shrubs: weigelas, forsythias, camellias
- Pinch out dahlia tips to encourage more growth
- Cut tatty leaves off alliums when yellow

## Harden off seedlings and plant out dahlias

When all risk of frost has gone – usually early May – it's time to start hardening seedlings off outdoors ready for planting on later in May by putting them outside during the day and bringing them in at night. You can also continue planting out dahlias into the garden as soon as the risk of frost has passed. If you use a greenhouse, monitor the internal temperatures and open air vents on warmer days.

## Harvest water

It can certainly feel like you've had your fair share of April showers, but have you been collecting rain runoff from your buildings? By installing a water butt, you can collect valuable rainwater now for use later in the summer, when wetter days are more sparse. With hosepipe bans the norm, you will want this lifeline for your plants.

Allow some of your grass to grow longer in May to encourage wildflowers to flourish.

## No Mow May

Your lawn is growing at a pace now, but step away from the lawnmower and allow grass to grow long for No Mow May (or at least designate a patch to it). By allowing the grass to grow longer, you give spring plants a chance to set seed before the first cut, allowing for healthier, more diverse lawns and providing vital nectar for bees, butterflies, and other pollinators.

## Chelsea chop

A certain flower show reminds us that this is a job for May. By chopping herbaceous perennials down, you can limit their size (and promote successional flowering) of many plants, such as *Nepeta*, asters, *Hylotelephium* (previously called *Sedum*), and phlox. Either cut the whole plant back by a third to promote shorter, bushier plants, or cut half of the plant back to encourage successional flowers.

# JUNE

Oh, June, you are glorious – flowers in abundance and the weather is usually at its best. The hard work of raising seedlings and planting out should be done, and it's a time to enjoy the fruits of your labour, so be sure to actually stop and enjoy the garden – this is it at its peak!

## TASKS THIS MONTH

- Sow biennials such as wallflowers and *Lunaria*
- Deadhead flowers for continuous blooms
- Thin out hardy annuals
- Reduce apples to 2–3 per cluster in late June
- Remove spring bulbs from pots and store
- Stake your dahlias to prevent them flopping
- Cut back your *Hylotelephium*
- Prune spring-flowering shrubs
- Prune box hedging and topiary

Keep deadheading repeat-flowering roses to ensure more blooms. Leave those that don't repeat flower to ensure you keep the rosehips for winter interest.

## Sow biennials

Wallflowers and *Lunaria* (honesty) are two of my favourites, and these need to be sown now to enjoy next year. You can sow directly outdoors or in pots if preferred – just be sure to plant into the final place in autumn.

## Deadhead spent flowers

Deadheading is vital if you want to ensure a long season of colour and a second (or third or more) flowering from your plants. All you need to do is snip off the flower heads of repeat flowering roses, perennials, and annuals to encourage the plant to produce more flowers. Try to snip to a leaf junction to keep things tidy. Also be sure you are harvesting your cut flowers and sweet peas as regularly as possible – more cutting leads to more flowers.

## Thin out annuals

Thinning out annuals is the process of pulling out seedlings to allow for plenty of space between plants. Most need about 30cm (12in) between each plant, so be merciless.

## Remove spring bulbs from pots

If you planted bulbs in pots, chances are the leaves have now turned yellow, and it's a good time to lift and store or compost them. I tend to compost tulip bulbs as they are never as good the following year, but if you have space, you can plant them in the ground come autumn. Narcissus, crocus, fritillaries, and others can be stored in a cool, dry spot to be planted in autumn.

## Cut back *Hylotelephium*

*Hylotelephium* has a habit of getting a bit gappy in the middle. Cut the plants back by a third to ensure bushier growth.

## Prune box hedging and topiary

If you still have box (*Buxus*) in the garden that has survived both box blight and box tree caterpillar, prune it in early June – if you do it any earlier, the leaves are still quite juvenile and more likely to bruise. To prevent the spread of blight, be sure to have a bucket of water with a little bleach in to sterilize the blades after pruning each plant.

# JULY

We're really in the thick of it now. If you've planned your planting carefully, your early summer planting should now be starting to hand over to the later summer interest. If it's all looking a bit tired out there, then now's a great time to take note and make a list of what to add in the autumn.

## TASKS THIS MONTH

- Feed roses and dahlias to encourage more blooms
- Prune wisteria again
- Pinch out annuals
- Thin out fruit on trees in early July
- Keep on top of deadheading
- Harvest lavender
- Clip yew
- Continue sowing biennials
- Cut back tired perennials for fresh growth
- Feed your containers

## Prune wisteria

At this point of the year, your wisteria is probably rather triffid like, with tendrils all over the place, in your gutters and covering windows. Prune it now to improve air circulation and let more sunlight into the plant, which is going to ensure you get a better flower show next year. Cut back the whippy green shoots to five or six buds, or 20cm (8in) from the main frame, to ensure the plant is focused on flower bud formation, not green growth.

Prune wisteria in January and July to keep it neat and to promote flowering.

## Thin fruit trees

Reduce apple and pear trees to two or three fruits per cluster. This is to ensure you get fewer, good-size fruits rather than many little tiddlers. It also prevents branches snapping from the weight of the fruit. Remove the smallest fruit and leave the largest to develop. You can also do this for plums, apricots, and peaches.

## Harvest lavender

Harvest lavender on a dry day and preferably in the morning, when the essential oils are at their best. Choose the newly opened stems for the best scent. Gather in bunches and hang to dry in a cool, dark place. We'll prune lavender further in August.

## Cut back tired perennials

Geraniums, *Nepeta*, and many other herbaceous perennials can look a bit tired by this point in the summer. Cut them back to the ground and they will reflush with fresh growth and more flowers.

*Nepeta* can be cut back hard in midsummer after flowering to promote further flowers and prevent it creating a gap in the centre.

# AUGUST

My birthday is in August and it always rains without fail! It's often a funny month of sunshine and showers, and deadheading is the name of the game this month to make sure your garden continues to work hard for you. It's often a time where we grow a little weary of this Sisyphean task, but keep going, and you'll have blooms until the frosts.

Despite it being high summer, it's not a busy time in the garden, in my view – other than watering and deadheading – so don't forget to just enjoy it! If you're headed away for a well-deserved break, be sure to pop any of the moisture-loving houseplants in the bath on a wet towel (yes, really) to make sure they don't dry out while you are away. You can also pop your sun-loving houseplants outdoors for their very own summer holiday.

## TASKS THIS MONTH

- Water camellias and rhododendrons
- Clip yew
- Deadhead and keep cutting those flowers
- Collect seeds
- Feed and water your containers
- Prune lavender
- Prune cherry, plum, magnolia, and walnut trees
- Prune wisteria, if you didn't do it last month

Keep picking dahlias to ensure blooms until the first frosts.

Prune lavender in August to prevent it getting woody.

## Water camellias and rhododendrons

August is the time when the new buds are forming for next year, so be sure they are well watered through this month to ensure the best display next year.

## Collect seeds

Now is a great time to collect ripe seeds and/or seedpods for sowing later. Pop your favourites in envelopes with a label and store somewhere cool and dry.

## Feed your containers

Watering and feeding containers are vital to ensure plants remain happy. Seaweed solution is a great feed, but check the needs of your individual plants.

## Prune lavender

If there is one thing I beg you to do this month, it's prune your lavender. If not pruned twice a year, lavender quickly becomes a woody, leggy mess. Trim back the new growth (green) to just above the old wood (brown). Be sure not to cut into old wood which can harm/kill the plant. You're aiming for a nice, neat mound at the end.

# SEPTEMBER

I love September, with the slight chill in the air hinting at an approaching autumn, but often providing us with some of the most perfect weather of the year. Nature's colour palette starts to turn golden, ochre, and deep red, with autumn fruits bursting to life. While we might not have had the long, hot summer we wished for, the usually high levels of rainfall across Britain have meant that our gardens have had a riotous few months.

September offers us plenty of good daylight hours to enjoy those happy late-summer plants in their prime, and get stuck into some proper gardening tasks, from dividing perennials to planting spring bulbs. Speaking of bulbs, have you ordered yours yet?

## TASKS THIS MONTH

- Lawn care
- Cut back any really tatty perennials
- Take cuttings of half-hardy plants
- Lift and divide perennials
  (see p169)
- Order spring bulbs
- Sow hardy annuals

## Lawn care

Some people have a real thing about the perfect lawn. If that's your jam, now is the time to scarify (break up mossy/weedy bits with a spiked tool called a scarifier), weed, and prepare the ground to reseed any bare patches.

## Tidy up perennials

Some herbaceous perennials (those that die back in winter and burst to life again in spring) will have finished flowering and may look a little scruffy by now. September is a good time to trim the scruffiest down to around ground level or a little above – you should see some new growth until the frosts. Just a note: don't hack down everything. I am a fan of leaving plenty for winter interest and wildlife, so just cut the really tatty ones.

Hardy geraniums are easy to divide. Simply dig them up with a spade and slice them in half or more, depending on their size, and replant.

## Take cuttings

You can take cuttings from half-hardy plants such as verbenas and salvias to produce many more plants (and we all love free plants). Cut an 8cm (3in) or so length of a non-flowering stem just below where a leaf emerges (called a node). Cut off any leaves below the top few and cut the growing tip off too. Pop it in a pre-watered pot of gritty, free-draining compost and leave to root in a cool greenhouse, on a windowsill, or even outside. In about three weeks, it will have rooted and you can pot on.

## Lift and divide perennials

Lift and divide congested clumps of perennials such as achilleas, geraniums, *Nepeta*, *Geum*, herbaceous peonies, *Dicentra*, and lily of the valley, among many others, once they finish flowering. See p169 for guidance on how to do this. Then replant in their new positions (preferably in groups of odd numbers – you know my feelings on planting single plants by now, darlings) with plenty of organic matter. Water well and await the pride and glory of creating free plants. Bravo.

## Order spring bulbs

Ah, it's that time of year when I start at a slow whisper in September and crescendo with an enormous shout in November of *order your bulbs!* Narcissus, tulips, *Galanthus* (snowdrops), fritillaries, hyacinths – you name it, get ordering.

SEPTEMBER                                                            179

# OCTOBER

I adore the light in October – that low-level sunlight filtering through the grasses and setting the oranges and reds of trees with fading leaves ablaze. There is so much to do in the garden in October, from sowing seeds to gathering leaves to make leaf mould, not to mention the dividing and moving of plants. If ever there was a time to go into overdrive in the garden, it is October.

## TASKS THIS MONTH

- Planting
- Gather and store fruit
- Sow hardy annuals
- Mulching
- Plant spring bulbs (except tulips)
- Prune evergreens
- Make leaf mould
- Lift and divide herbaceous perennials (see p169)
- Resist the urge to cut everything back
- Plant indoor bulbs such as paperwhites and *Hippeastrum* for Christmas flowering

## Planting

With the soil still warm, now is the time to get planting so that roots have time to establish before the cold weather hits. This means your plants get a head start for next year and hit the ground running. Towards the end of the month if it's cold enough, bare-root season commences, meaning it's a great time to buy hedging, shrubs, trees, and roses, which arrive as a root ball or bare root, rather than potted.

## Harvest fruit

Now is the time to think about any fruit trees or bushes you want to plant. British fruit really comes into its own in autumn, such as apples and pears and the odd plum. If you are already blessed with a glut of ripe apples, store any perfect ones in a cool, dark place and pray to the mouse gods that they aren't found.

## Sow hardy annuals

Sow hardy annuals seeds such as scabious, *Nigella damascena* 'Miss Jekyll', and *Ammi majus* to overwinter and germinate in colder conditions.

## Mulching

Mulching improves the condition of your soil, suppresses weeds as we head into rainier seasons (and retains water in drier ones), and protects roots – so many wins. Don't be shy, 5–8cm (2–3in) of mulch needs to go around all the beds, but just be careful not to smother small plants or heap against the stems of large ones. Leave any drought-tolerant Mediterranean plants as they won't fare well with additional retained moisture.

## Plant spring bulbs

Plant up your spring bulbs into containers, *except* tulips – hold fire until it starts to get frosty in November/December. This reduces their risk of disease from the soil and increases the chance of the magnificent tulip display you are waiting for.

## Make leaf mould

Regularly gather autumn leaves into jute bags, loosely tied black bin liners, or repurposed old compost bags with holes poked in them. These can be hidden away for one to two years, after which they will have formed the most wonderful mulch.

## Leave the skeletons

Remember to leave some spent flowers and seedheads (such as hydrangeas, *Echinacea*, *Phlomis*, *Eryngium*, and *Echinops*) for structural interest and for food and shelter for birds and insects over the winter. You don't want to cut everything to the ground and be left with swathes of bare earth.

A "bulb lasagne" in a container will provide a long display of spring flowers. Plant the largest bulbs at the bottom and add compost for each layer, with the smallest bulbs at the top of the container.

# NOVEMBER

Leaves are falling, fires look very tempting, and knitwear and boots are on. Some plants may be having a last hurrah of flowers before the hard frosts, so enjoy their efforts and leave any lovely skeletons for winter structure.

And now to more pressing matters – bulbs, have you ordered yours? Or maybe even started to plant some too? When nighttime temperatures are consistently below 10°C (50°F), you can start planting your tulips, but don't worry – you have all of November and December (and even January at a push). It's also time to plant bare-root shrubs and roses and move anything that's been bothering you.

## TASKS THIS MONTH

- Plant spring bulbs
- Tool husbandry
- Lift and store dahlias
- Plant trees, shrubs, and bare-root roses and hedges

## Plant spring bulbs

Bulbs, bulbs, bulbs, I love bulbs. And you will too if you plant enough of them now. Go ahead and plant pots, borders, and your lawn with bulbs now for a spectacular spring show. You can also start looking at bulbs to plant for indoor Christmas decorations or gifts.

## Tool husbandry

As most of the garden goes into hibernation, it's good to give your tools a little TLC. Clean off any mud, dunk hand tools in a vinegar and water mix, and scrub with stainless steel pads to remove any rust or use a scouring block like Crean Mate. Give tools a sharpen and use specialist oil to give a protective coating to stave off rust, before storing them somewhere dry ready for a new season of work come spring.

## Lift and store dahlias

Dahlias don't reliably survive the British winter in the ground, so it is best to lift and store the tubers. Once the foliage has started to die off, carefully dig around and lift the tubers with a fork. Gently shake off the soil, cut off the leaves, and brush off any remaining soil. When dry, pack in a box or pot with dry compost or in dry newspaper and leave them in a dry, frost-free place until the frosts are over in spring. If you live in the south and your dahlias are in a warm, sheltered spot, you can just cut back the stems and add a thick layer of mulch over the top to protect them, but this is a gamble.

## Planting

If the ground isn't frozen or waterlogged, now is the perfect time to plant trees, shrubs, bare-root roses, and hedges. You can also continue to move or divide herbaceous perennials (see p169) and take hardwood cuttings of shrubs.

November is the month to lift your dahlia tubers and store them in a dry, frost-free place for the winter.

# DECEMBER

December is the month when, frankly, gardening is at the bottom of most of our to-do lists. It's cold, dark, and wet, but I do like to venture outside to snip buckets of evergreens to bring inside for a little festive cheer. It's also a great time to snatch some quiet moments to put any remaining spring bulbs in the ground – I tend to save it for the quiet days after Christmas when time stands still.

If you want to start planning for next year, now's a great time to start browsing seed catalogues ready to start sowing in the new year, and you can always plant paperwhites and other indoor-flowering bulbs to bring the outdoors in.

## TASKS THIS MONTH

- Tree pruning
- Feed the birds
- Sweep leaves away from pathways
- Check your boundaries
- Sow sweet peas
- Continue to plant trees, shrubs, and bare-root roses

## Tree pruning

Now is the perfect time to study your deciduous trees from all angles, consider their form and size, and give them a prune. Pruning keeps them healthy and controls their size, and winter is the time to do it. Remove any dead, damaged, or diseased branches first. Then remove any weak growth or any that would be better removed to give a more pleasing shape. Limit pruning to no more than about a fifth of the tree canopy in one year. Save pruning of cherry, plum, magnolia, and walnut trees until spring and summer.

## Feed the birds

Our little feathered friends start to struggle with food at this time of year, so hang bird feeders and replenish and clean them regularly. Attracting birds to your garden in winter means that when the weather warms next year, they will still be visiting and eating pests as your plants start their growing season again. Keep birdbaths topped up so birds can regulate the oil on their feathers and therefore their temperature. Clear out any nest boxes so mites and parasites cannot grow, and birds looking for a prospective new home in January will be safe and happy.

Sow sweet peas in late December for an early flush of blooms the following year.

## Sweep, sweep, sweep

Leaf sweeping is a Sisyphean task, but do persevere. The last few leaves floating from the trees can be left in a pile in case hedgehogs or other creatures use them to hibernate over winter. Avoid forking over your compost heap in case hedgehogs, reptiles, amphibians, or bees have decided to take shelter.

## Check your boundaries

With many plants dormant at the moment, it is a good time to check your fences, trellis, or other timber structures to see if repairs or even replacements are needed. Save any painting for when temperatures exceed 5°C (41°F).

## Sow sweet peas

Sowing sweet peas in December will result in earlier blooms – you can always plant more in January and February for a succession, but this is a task I ritualistically do on Boxing Day. You can sow sweet peas under cover now: plant two seeds in peat-free multipurpose compost in cardboard loo rolls to facilitate a deep, narrow root run. Allow them to germinate on a warm windowsill, in a heated propagator, or in a gently heated greenhouse.

# RESOURCES

## Retail nurseries

**Beth Chatto**
bethchatto.co.uk

**Claire Austin**
claireaustin-hardyplants.co.uk

**David Austin Roses**
davidaustinroses.co.uk

**Form Plants**
formplants.com

**Hardy's Cottage Garden Plants**
hardysplants.co.uk

## Trees

**Barcham Trees**
barcham.co.uk

**Deepdale Trees**
deepdale-trees.co.uk

**Majestic Trees**
majestictrees.co.uk

## Bulbs

**Crocus**
crocus.co.uk

**Farmer Gracy**
farmergracy.co.uk

**Jacques Amand International**
jacquesamandintl.com

**J. Parker's**
jparkers.co.uk

**Sarah Raven**
sarahraven.com

## Seeds

**Chiltern Seeds**
chilternseeds.co.uk

**Sarah Raven**
sarahraven.com

## Decking

**Champion Timber**
championtimber.com

**Jewson**
jewson.co.uk

**Millboard**
millboard.com

## Fencing

**Jacksons Fencing**
jacksons-fencing.co.uk

**The Garden Trellis Company**
gardentrellis.co.uk

## Paving

**All Green**
allgreen.uk

**Artorius Faber**
artoriusfaber.com

**CED Stone**
cedstone.co.uk

**London Stone**
londonstone.co.uk

**Schellevis**
schellevis.nl

**Vande Moortel**
vandemoortel.co.uk

## Lighting

**Collingwood**
collingwoodlighting.com

**Hunza Lighting**
hunzalighting.com

**Landscape Plus**
landscapeplus.com

## Pizza ovens and kamados

**Big Green Egg**
biggreenegg.co.uk

**Gozney**
gozney.com

**Ooni Pizza Ovens**
uk.ooni.com

## Pots

**Pots & Pithoi**
potsandpithoi.com

**Torc Pots**
torcpots.com

## Sheds

**The Cosy Shed Company**
thecosyshedco.co.uk

**The Posh Shed Company**
theposhshedcompany.co.uk

# INDEX

Page numbers in **bold** refer
to illustrations

## Author's acknowledgements

When I was little and my grandmother came to visit, the first order of business would be for her and my father to walk around the garden for a thorough inspection of what was thriving and what wasn't doing quite so well. My grandmother loved gardening, she had the gardener's dream – a walled garden that she generously opened to the public. It's a cruel irony that I fell in love with gardening too late to share my passion with her, but I am happy to report that the baton of the garden inspection with my father has been handed on to me. She has been in my mind as I write this – thank you, Grandma.

To my parents, thank you for your unwavering support and pride. I love you bags and bags.

To my team, thank you for putting up with me, for being my sounding boards, consultants, snack partners, agony aunts, and generally brilliant people to work alongside.

To my glorious team at DK: Lucy, Barbara, Ruth, Chris, Dawn, and Geoff, thank you for shepherding me through this terrifying process and making it all feel so easy. And to Rachel for your beautiful photography, you are a master.

To my darling C, let's grow things together, always.

## Publisher's acknowledgements

DK would like to thank Grade Design for initial designs; Rituraj Singh for picture research; Kathryn Glendenning for the proofread; Ruth Ellis for the index; and Adam Brackenbury for repro work.

## Picture credits

The publisher would like to thank the following for their kind permission to reproduce their photographs:

(Key: a–above; b–below/bottom; c–centre; f–far; l–left; r–right; t–top)

4 Rachel Warne. 14 Rachel Warne: (tr). 25 Pollyanna Wilkinson: (cl, bl, tc). 34 Alamy Stock Photo: Premium Stock Photography GmbH/Frank Teigler (bc). 35 Alamy Stock Photo: shapencolour (br). 37 Pollyanna Wilkinson: (br). 51 Pollyanna Wilkinson. 52–53 Pollyanna Wilkinson: (tl). 61 Rachel Warne. 70 GAP Photos: Designer: Adam Woolcott and Jonathan Smith. Sponsor: The Garden Centre Group (br). 71 GAP Photos: (tl); Stephen Studd (tr). 72 GAP Photos: Richard Bloom (tl); Richard Bloom – Designer: Craig Reynolds (cl); Lee Avison – Garden Design: Angie Barker, Garden Design for All Seasons (bl). 74 Pollyanna Wilkinson: (bl). 75 GAP Photos: Elke Borkowski (cr). 76 GAP Photos: Lynn Keddie – Designer: Charlotte Harris – Sponsor: RBC (tl); Marianne Majerus Garden Images: Bennet Smith (bl). 78 GAP Photos: Global Stone Paving (bc); Stephen Studd (bl). 81 Dreamstime.com: Radoslav Cajkovic (b); GAP Photos: Mandy Bradshaw (tl). 82 Pollyanna Wilkinson: (bl, tr). 85 Shutterstock.com: Douglas Cliff (cr); Cre8 design (br). Pollyanna Wilkinson: (bl). 86–87 Rachel Warne: (t). 88 GAP Photos: Juliette Wade – Designer Freddy Whyte/Brampton Willows (bl). 91 GAP Photos: (tr, br). Pollyanna Wilkinson: (bl). 117 Rachel Warne: (t). 119 Pollyanna Wilkinson: (t). 124–25 Rachel Warne: (br). 129 Pollyanna Wilkinson: (br). 137 GAP Photos: Howard Rice – Wynyard Hall Rose Garden, Stockton-on-Tees (br). 140–41 Pollyanna Wilkinson: (tr). 153 Alamy Stock Photo: Jacky Parker (bl); P Tomlins (tc). Dreamstime.com: Simona Pavan (crb). 154 Alamy Stock Photo: Botany vision (crb). 155 Alamy Stock Photo: Tim Gainey (cra); Deborah Vernon (crb). 157 Katie Spicer: (tr). 158 Pollyanna Wilkinson. 163 Pollyanna Wilkinson: (tr). 164 Alamy Stock Photo: The National Trust Photolibrary (b). 167 Alamy Stock Photo: Deborah Vernon (t). 169 Pollyanna Wilkinson: (tr). 172 Pollyanna Wilkinson: (bl). 174 Pollyanna Wilkinson: (br). 176 Alamy Stock Photo: shapencolour (bl). 177 Alamy Stock Photo: Denis Crawford (tr). 179 GAP Photos: (t). 180 Pollyanna Wilkinson: (tr). 183 Pollyanna Wilkinson: (b). 185 Alamy Stock Photo: Deborah Vernon (tr). 192 Katie Spicer: (tl).

All other images © Dorling Kindersley Limited

*To my boys, Leo and Raf, you are the best things I have ever grown.*

## About the author

Pollyanna Wilkinson is an award-winning garden designer and founder and creative director of her landscape design studio, Studio Pollyanna. The studio strives to create elegant, liveable, and biodiverse gardens across the UK and overseas.

Before her career in garden design, Polly worked in marketing before realizing that she craved a more creative path. She retrained in garden design, graduating with distinction from the English Gardening School at the Chelsea Physic Garden, and set up the studio shortly after.

As well as designing gardens for private and commercial clients, Polly has designed show gardens for RHS Chelsea Flower Show and RHS Hampton Court Palace Garden Festival. She holds two coveted People's Choice awards, most recently for her Mothers for Mothers garden at RHS Chelsea in 2022. She also has a silver-gilt and two silver medals.

You can find Polly on Instagram @pollyanna_wilkinson, where she shares gardening and design expertise.

**Editorial Manager** Ruth O'Rourke
**Project Editor** Lucy Philpott
**Senior Designer** Barbara Zuniga
**DTP and Design Coordinator** Heather Blagden
**Production Editor** David Almond
**Senior Production Controller** Samantha Cross
**Jacket and Sales Material Coordinator**
Emily Cannings
**Art Director** Maxine Pedliham

**Editorial** Dawn Titmus
**Design** Geoff Borin
**Illustration** Stuart Jackson-Carter
**Photography** Rachel Warne
**Consultant Gardening Publisher** Chris Young

First published in Great Britain in 2025 by
Dorling Kindersley Limited
20 Vauxhall Bridge Road,
London SW1V 2SA

The authorized representative in the EEA is
Dorling Kindersley Verlag GmbH. Arnulfstr. 124,
80636 Munich, Germany

A CIP catalogue record for this book
is available from the British Library.
ISBN: 978-0-2416-4881-0

Printed and bound in China

**www.dk.com**

MIX
Paper | Supporting
responsible forestry
FSC™ C018179

This book was made with Forest Stewardship Council™ certified paper – one small step in DK's commitment to a sustainable future.
**Learn more at www.dk.com/uk/information/sustainability**